The ABC Complete Book
of School Marketing

The ABC Series

The ABC Complete Book of School Marketing

The ABC Complete Book of School Surveys

The ABCs of Teacher Marketing

The ABCs of School Board Marketing

The ABC Complete Book of School Marketing

William J. Banach

The Scarecrow Press, Inc.
A Scarecrow Education Book
Lanham, Maryland, and London
2001

SCARECROW PRESS, INC.
A Scarecrow Education Book

Published in the United States of America
by Scarecrow Press, Inc.
4720 Boston Way, Lanham, Maryland 20706
www.scarecroweducation.com

4 Pleydell Gardens, Folkestone
Kent CT20 2DN, England

British Library Cataloguing in Publication Information Available

Library of Congress Cataloging-in-Publication Data
Banach, William Joseph.
    The ABC complete book of school marketing / William J. Banach.—2nd ed.
        p. cm. — (A Scarecrow education book)
    ISBN 0-8108-3947-4 (pbk. : alk. paper)
    1. Schools—Marketing—Handbooks, manuals, etc. 2. Educational
planning—Handbooks, manuals, etc. I. Title. II. Series.
    LB2847 .B367 2001
    371.2'07—dc21   00-067122

⊖™The paper used in this publication meets the minimum requirements of American National Standard for Information Sciences—Permanence of Paper for Printed Library Materials, ANSI/NISO Z39.48-1992. Manufactured in the United States of America.

Contents

Contents continued

Welcome to the world of radical change

Welcome to the world of radical change!

People say things are different today. They're right! Things are *radically* different than they were just a few years ago.

The forces of radical change have taken us beyond the limits of our education and experience. These forces cause us to look at the change around us and admit that, "We never learned about *this* in school." Or, they lead us to search for answers in our memory and confess that, "We've never seen *anything* like this before."

Radical change has deposited us at a frontier where there are few, if any, guideposts. The rules have changed and the new rule book is just being drafted!

Radical change has implications for every individual and every organization. No person and no organization is immune. A report from the Pew Charitable Trust says it directly:

No institution will emerge unscathed
from its confrontation with an external environment
that is substantially altered and in many ways more hostile.

How radical change affects public education

The forces of radical change have generated substantial turbulence for public education.

▮ First, *the level of public confidence is continually in question* as people who face uncertainty in their own lives and organizations focus their attention on schools.

In a way, it seems, people are searching for someone or something to blame for the discomforts they are experiencing as a result of radical change. Whatever the reasons, public confidence in public education is not what educators would like it to be.

- Second, *the political environment for public education is not positive.* The news media and the business community continually call for changes in the public educational system. Their concerns and unflattering accusations have resulted in a public agenda which has educational reform near the top. And, because no politician wants an angry constituency, legislators are advancing initiatives -- such as parental choice, educational charters, vouchers, and tax credits -- to address the perceived ills of public education.

  The common denominator in these politically driven initiatives is that they tend to be quick fixes. There also is a lack evidence to indicate that they will serve learners more effectively than public schools over the long haul. Nonetheless, as a result of radical change, many people want to try something different because they perceive the current system to be dysfunctional.

- Third, *the demographic make-up and psychographic composition of the public are changing.* It's been a long time since parents were the majority in our neighborhoods. Our communities have more interest groups now. Leadership is continually questioned ... and doubted. And the macro forces driving consumption are speed, value, convenience, customer service, and price.

  One result of these changes is that mustering simple majorities in support of public education is not a simple task any more. In an educational marketplace characterized by multiple options, the question people are asking is, "Who can teach me -- at a decent price for value received -- what I want to know when I want to know it?"

- Fourth, *technology has emerged as an educational wild card.* The home is already the largest U.S. market for educational technology. Technology is simultaneously becoming more sophisticated, less expensive, and easier to use. Further, communication technology companies are buying content-rich companies, posturing for market leadership in the knowledge age. They are targeting the home market, and their products and services are creating a learning society.

All these forces will enhance the educational options people already have, and they will make new choices available to them.

Parents, for example, have always had the right to choose a public, private, or parochial school education for their children, and the legislation which allows parents to choose which public school their children will attend is already on the books in many states. The concept of parental choice has widespread political appeal. But now a variety of advocates are seeking public financial support for private and parochial schools, and many legislators are responding to their requests by providing funding for the full spectrum of choice initiatives.

One theory central to educational choice is that marketplace demand will strengthen good schools while simultaneously putting bad schools out of business. Whether you agree with this theory or not, choice legislation indeed changes the educational marketplace.

The new marketplace, no doubt, will be characterized by more educational options -- from technology-driven networking to corporate learning programs to self-instruction. This means education will be driven by economics because, sooner or later, at least some portion of state and federal funding will follow students to the educational option they choose. The movement from an information-based economy to a knowledge-based economy will solidify economics -- not societal needs or political response -- as the driving force behind education. Economics, in fact, is now making learning the business of business.

How choices will be made

We live in a fast-paced society that is populated by increasingly sophisticated people. These two characteristics will combine to influence customer behavior and decision-making.

The availability of educational information and the growing sophistication of consumers enables learners (and/or their parents) to exercise choices on the basis of speed, value, convenience, customer service, and price.

However, education is a complex enterprise, and many learners (and/or their parents) will not take the time to study its components before making a choice. Their decisions will be based largely on perceptions. And, while more people may depend on perceptions than on educational reality, educators will have to be concerned with both groups.

On one hand, even the best school in the world will have difficulty functioning if people don't know about it or if they don't perceive it as a quality institution. On the other hand, positive perceptions must be reinforced by educational effectiveness because poor performance destroys positive perceptions.

How *The ABC Complete Book of School Marketing* will help you

We designed this workbook to help you function in an educational marketplace that is characterized by multiple options. It can help you make your school a viable choice by giving you a process which improves educational quality *and* public perceptions. We call this process The Market-Driven System® (The MDS).

The Market-Driven System® will help you develop a master plan for your school district. It is an umbrella concept that complements virtually all educational initiatives. It is, in fact, a process that will help you coordinate and enhance your continuous efforts to improve your schools. And it will help you capitalize on change.

The Market-Driven System® is also a site-based process that enables your staff to coordinate myriad change activities at the building, department, and classroom levels. The process will help everyone travel in the direction of your school district's vision. It will also give you strategic guidance for planning at all levels, and it will ensure that the change priorities you identify are consistent with the mission of your school.

In this workbook, you'll learn about the nature of change, its dimensions, and its implications. You'll learn how to listen to people and engage them in your planning. And you'll learn about the concepts of marketing, targeting, and positioning, and how you can use these concepts to build a marketing program.

We've even included a case study, examples of a marketing program in action, and all the forms you need to create an effective plan for your school district.

Perspectives on planning and marketing

Perspectives on planning and marketing

The Market-Driven System® is an adaptable process that combines the concepts of strategic thinking, planning, and marketing. It was designed to create effective, future-oriented organizations while building marketplace support for them. Speed, simplicity, and practicality characterize The MDS process.

If you follow The MDS process, you'll help your organization avoid planning paralysis by moving quickly from the planning stage to actually *doing* something to create the future that you envision.

The MDS process addresses the complexities of systematic change. It also gives you the mechanisms for involving key stakeholders without getting bogged down in endless studies, reports and mind-numbing minutia.

At the same time, The MDS process reduces uncertainty because it helps you:

- accommodate the forces of radical change;
- create a responsive, future-focused organization; and,
- provide a framework through which you can coordinate other continuous improvement initiatives.

On the following pages, we'll give you more details about The MDS process and show you how it can work for you.

The MDS process is a cycle with five steps:

1. *Analyze* the environment in which your organization functions. This is the first and most important step in the process. It is also the most frequently ignored.

2. *Strategize* how to accommodate what the analysis reveals.

3. Write a *plan.* Develop goals and objectives and specify *who* is going to do *what* by *when.*
(Remember, if your plan is not in writing, you really don't have a plan!)

4. *Execute* the plan. Do what the plan says should be done.

5. *Evaluate* the results. Assess the factors that lead you to attain or not attain your goals.

If you think about it, this basic model can be the model for anything. It makes sense as a model for planning, marketing, change ... common sense. And that's the point. The MDS is a common sense model, and it is critically important to the success of your planning, marketing and change initiatives.

Before you begin, note these critical caveats

Before you start planning and marketing, consider these important points:

■ *There is never an ideal time to start planning, nor is there an ideal implementation sequence.*

The year is half over ... the budget has already been established ... the organization already has goals -- but no vision ... the organization already has a vision -- but no goals ... any excuse to delay planning will do.

The trick is to jump into the process and, over time, get the planning, budgeting, marketing, and all the other organization processes into synch.

■ *The process is cyclical.* The five-step process begins with analyzing and ends with evaluating, and evaluation provides the transition to the beginning of a new cycle in which you reanalyze environment, recheck strategy, and revise the plan.

■ *Don't think of a plan; think of a planning process.* When planning ends, obsolescence begins. Accommodating radical change requires that you make the planning process a way of doing business. Here's why: The effectiveness of any organization is directly related to the quality of the knowledge that it prossesses. But new discoveries are being made continuously and new information is being generated in unprecedented quantity. Things are changing and it's inevitable that the things that are changing will affect your plan. That's precisely why you have to keep processing the plan.

Here's an analogy to underline the point: You can develop a flight plan from Minneapolis to Memphis today, but you can't fly the flight plan next month. In fact, you can't even fly it tomorrow. Why? For one thing, weather conditions change rapidly. It may be sunny in Minneapolis today, but snowy tomorrow. The jet stream may move north and pick up speed, or turbulence may exist at different altitudes. A whole host of variables could change and make your flight plan obsolete.

So, with all these variables in play all the time, how do airplanes manage to get from here to there? It's easy -- pilots process their plans. Their guidance systems monitor environmental factors that need to be accommodated by computer, by the pilot, or by both. So, while a pilot may start with a plan for getting to a destination, to have a successful flight, the plan has to be processed all along the way. Remember that the Apollo missions to the moon were off-course 90% of the time. Computers -- and astronauts -- monitored data from guidance systems and made continuing mid-course corrections.

Educational planning is analogous to flight planning. While a plan is absolutely essential, it won't get you to your destination unless you process it.

■ *Every step in the process is important.* Make sure that you follow every step in the process -- in the appropriate order. Leaving out steps can create problems that may adversely affect the planning process. So, remember ...

If you do everything except this...	Odds are, you'll wind up...
analyze	misdirected
strategize	overwhelmed
plan	aimless
execute	frustrated
evaluate	uncertain

■ *Involving people is critical.*

If you want commitment, you'll have to involve people.
People need to be involved in decisions that affect their destiny.
If you want people to be part of the plan, you have to make them part of the process.

These declarations aren't new , yet we continue to ignore them. Effective schools and proactive plans for the future result from having a process for working toward your vision -- and the process must involve key stakeholders.

Process is central to The Market-Driven System®. Anyone can write a plan and develop a checklist of activities. But, if you impose your plan without eliciting input, you should expect a less than enthusiastic reception. Ideally, you should involve everyone who will be affected by your plan. When the realities of logistics make this impossible make sure that all your stakeholders are at least represented in the process.

■ *Make something happen ... fast.* The last thing people need is
another series of meetings. Your success in creating change will
be directly related to the enthusiasm that you bring to the effort
and what you produce. Don't spend months gearing up to plan.
As you initiate the planning process, take pains to produce
something that people can point to -- something that indicates
progress on the path toward the future.

As an example, make creating a vision for your school a priority.
When it's finished, disseminate it widely.   Post it in the foyer.
Print it in all your publications. Use it in your speeches and refer
to it in conversations with your staff. In short, let people know
that you are committed to taking action. Give them progress that
they can see, touch, or hear.

■ *Champion the change.* Your use of the vision statement is an
example of championing the change. *You* will have to facilitate the
planning process and *you* will have to keep the process on the
agenda. This may be the most difficult part of the process. Because enthusiasm eventually wanes and people have a tendency to
seek new agendas.

If you think strategically, you can generate new information,
recycle the knowledge gained from experience, and put a new spin
on things. You must relate all this, however, to the five-step
planning process and the vision, mission, and change priorities
it produces.

Do what you can to make any new agenda a part of The MDS
process.   (The same is true for new events, issues, and
opportunities. You must evaluate them within the context of the
planning process. For example, consider a new assessment
program within the context of your school's vision, mission, and
goals. If the assessment program is consistent with your direction,
you should accommodate it. If it isn't, communicate the fact that it
is inconsistent with your direction and move on.)

■ *Attitudes may need to be adjusted.* The process for change that we outline in this workbook may require some attitude changes. The Market-Driven System® is a customer-oriented process and it depends heavily on schools and the people they serve having a strong partnership. For this partnership to be successful, your staff and the other people in the process will need to understand different points of view and exhibit a collaborative spirit.

Most school people are not used to working in a competitive environment. They may not readily understand the importance of seeing things from the customer's point of view. In fact, they may not view customer service as something that should concern them.

Some educators may not realize that your customers have other educational options that they can exercise. Your staff needs to know that "lack of concern" and "negative employee contacts" are the prime reasons people take their business elsewhere. Given choice in a school environment, the existence of these negatives can adversely affect your market.

Still other people may try to accommodate radical change by denying that it exists at all. These people often cope with change by deceiving themselves about its existence or impact.

Now that you've had an overview of The Market-Driven System®, in the next three sections of the workbook, we'll ask some fundamental questions and discuss change forces and their implications.

What's *an education*... and where's its constituency?

What's *an education*
... and where's its constituency?

If you think about it, there's a simple reason for many of the dilemmas facing public education: most educators can't explain what *an education* is. Nor can most parents, business people, community leaders, and politicians. And even if they could, each of them would probably define it differently!

This predicament leads to predictable results: with increasing frequency educators are frustrated, citizens are upset, business people grow impatient, politicians push quick fixes ... and students are short-changed.

That's why educators need to take the lead, engage people in dialogue, and define what *an education* is, community by community, all across America. And then they need to build a constituency for the education they define, community by community, all across America.

Everyone knows education is important: "You won't get anywhere without *an education*," they say. "You have to have *an education*. There's nothing more important than *an education*." But most people can't tell you what *an education* is.

Yet, most people have opinions about what an education ought to be. Typically, they express these opinions by using a component of the educational process to explain what an education *is not*. "An education *is not* this subject or that subject or this outcome or that outcome or this book or that book," they say.

But the fact remains, when pressed to think systemically and consider the learning process in its entirety, most people can't tell you what an education *is*.

So, what is *an education*?

Education is a process. It acquires definition when it's placed on a continuum. And, it evolves to something better only when it's considered systemically, in context, and -- perhaps -- over a lifetime.

People in some communities might define *an education* as reading, writing, and arithmetic -- the 3 Rs. This definition might place them between zero and three on a ten-point "educational continuum." People in other communities might define *an education* more broadly. Their definition might place them around four or five on the ten-point continuum.

Regardless of how people define an education, it's likely they will find themselves shy of point ten on the continuum. That's one of the most beneficial reasons for engaging people in defining the dimensions of an education. People learn where their community is and where it is likely to go. They come to consensus on what they want from their schools. And they begin to discover what it will take to get where they want to go.

Think of the value of knowing these things! This is information leaders can use to help people develop broader perspectives as they discover other possibilities on the continuum. This is information leaders can use to more effectively deploy their strategic communication resources. This is information leaders can use to build a constituency which will help move a community in the direction of ten.

Defining an education produces these outcomes

- As people define an education, they define themselves. And as people define what education can become, they define their aspirations. The more everyone learns what everyone else believes and wants, the easier it is to address concerns, come to consensus, and build coalitions for change.

- By coming to consensus on what an education is, educators and community members take the first step toward building a supportive constituency for schools. They also begin to learn that education cannot be the sole responsibility of educators. Rather, they discover that a quality educational program requires assumption of responsibility by everyone in the community.

■ Knowing how an education is defined enables educators to effectively install change strategies and develop on-target communication. It means marketers can do a better job of providing the school information people need and want. And it means that while some people may mount a campaign to raise community expectations and school performance, others might leave to search for more fertile soil when they learn that their community is content with mediocrity and mired in the past.

How to get started defining an education and building a constituency

1. Commit to defining what an education is and what it can become.

While its seems obvious that educators should know what an education is, that's not always the case. Many educators (and parents and business people and politicians) focus on a component of the educational system instead of the big picture. That's because it's easier to isolate a part of the system, define what's wrong with it, try to fix it, and then stuff it back into the system.

But systems theory tells us that every system -- including the educational system -- is a product of the interaction of its parts. You cannot deal with individual parts in isolation because each part affects the performance of the whole. Yet, that's what many people do. In fact, school improvement initiatives often are designed to identify parts of the system that aren't working. Those parts (reading, math, science, etc.) are then pulled from the system for improvement and, eventually, reinstalled in the system ... without regard to the impact any changes might have on other parts of the system.

In their pursuit of quick fixes, some people adversely affect the entire educational system by focusing on a *piece* of a part. This is easier still, and it makes for great headlines! That's why critics and politicians, particularly, pick at specific educational outcomes and programs, or commonly held perceptions such as the need to "cut the fat" or "administrative accountability." The result of picking things apart or reconfiguring them one piece at a time is that few things change and -- in the end -- the result is not an effective educational system, but a collection of pieces that don't mesh.

Inability to define an education makes schools vulnerable to the whims of every interest group. And it may be a root cause of superintendents getting fired and communities being nonplussed with their school boards.

2. *Understand that communication is the essence of building constituencies.*

Management guru Peter Drucker says that communication is the essence of organization. It is also the essence of building coalitions.

You can't build and sustain a constituency for an educational program -- or anything else -- without dialogue that is open, systemic, two-way, and honest. Here the idea is not to tell people what an education is, but to help them see what they haven't seen before, to engage them in discussion, to listen to their needs and wants, to create an educational vision, and to join hands in pursuing it.

Trying to build coalitions without communication is like trying to eat without food. It simply can't be done.

3. *Identify the societal context and critical issues external to and within your community.*

Major demographic shifts, technological advances and discoveries, and entrepreneurs are prime drivers of radical change. They, in turn, are producing a new context for life itself. This context shapes the environment in which an educational system must function. And performing in this new context is what produces dilemmas and issues for leaders.

As an example, take one dimension of the emerging context: workforce transformation. It's obvious that the nature of the American workforce is changing. Farm workers were replaced by factory laborers. Next came growth in the service sector, and now we're just beginning to define what we have and where we're headed.

We are on a course that will produce a bifurcated workforce. Well educated people will populate one end of the workforce continuum. Their ranks and their relative affluence are growing. At the other end of the continuum will be those characterized by less education. Their ranks are growing but their relative affluence is shrinking. Hence, it seems that an education is one key to being on the money end of the job market continuum.

But relationships between people and organizations also are changing the world of work. For example, today there are more contingency workers -- people who are employed to do what needs to be done. Once their assignment is complete, they move on to the next assignment or employer.

The movement toward contingency workers is being driven by technology, the nature of change, and the costs of employing people. Technology brings productive capacity to the contingent worker. The nature of change creates the contingent worker's market. The more current one stays in a period of radical change, the more employable that individual is. And the cost of having employees (such as fringe benefits, retirement programs, government mandates, legal requirements, and sundry other human resource obligations) makes it easier and more profitable for companies to look for solid, short-term relationships instead of long-term marriages.

Given that this is happening and given that some forecasters are now predicting that the typical American will have four-to-seven careers and ten or more jobs over the course of a lifetime (half of which do not now exist!), it makes sense to ask, "What should an education prepare students to become?"

Discussion about matters like these dictates that communities come together, learn about the changing context and the issues it is producing, and think about implications. Then dialogue can lead to informed decisions about what role all members of a community must play in the development of young people and their future.

4. Broaden horizons by helping people appreciate the inherent excitement of learning and the myriad options which exist on the educational continuum.

Everyone knows what it feels like to *catch on* -- to know that you know. People need to be reminded of the ecstasy of learning and the self-satisfaction it brings. Ask them to recall those enlightening moments, and help them understand how an education can continue turning on lights. Once they learn that they'll begin to explore the endless options on the educational continuum from a more positive perspective.

5. *Help people identify barriers and enablers.*

People can move from where they are to where they want to be if they learn how to overcome barriers and capitalize on the forces compelling change. When people decide to move beyond where they are on the continuum, it's important that they develop strategies related to: 1. the barriers that have potential for preventing change, for keeping them stuck in the status quo; and, 2. the enablers, the things that will help them get where they want to go.

Once the barriers and enablers are identified, the change strategy can become focused. People can decide how to eliminate or accommodate barriers. And, they can decide what actions they should take to unleash the enablers.

6. *Develop the facilitation skills of anyone who wants to lead anything.*

In a period of radical change no one person or group has all the answers. (This is something that's unchanged!) That's why dialogue, communication, collaboration, and consensus-building are critical. But these processes have to be facilitated.

Everyone knows that involving people in educational decision-making is important. People need forums where they can present their point of view while learning the viewpoints of others. Good facilitators make this process work. They create understanding and consensus through dialogue and discussion.

Facilitating is a learned skill, yet there are few places to learn it. Perhaps that's why too many decisions take too long and result in too many people feeling as if they've wasted too much time.

7. *Understand that education and change are both complex processes, and that you can only make a difference if your perspective is broad, systemic, and long-term.*

Recent research on change and systems confirms what we already knew -- large scale change is very complex and it takes a long time. That's why leaders often leave before change is complete and dreams are fulfilled.

The best gifts any leader can give any organization are vision and process. Vision provides direction for the entire system, and process provides continuity.

Both vision and continuity are longer-lasting than leaders. That's one reason those who want to see their dreams fulfilled must translate them into a vision and install a systemic process which will sustain the pursuit of priorities.

This is a period of complex, accelerating, radical change. That means it cannot be a time of linear, incremental response. It also means that the educational enterprise must seek, embrace, and protect players who can bring the new perspectives and brighter promise of vision and process.

As the often-quoted African proverb says, it takes a whole village to educate a child. If that's the case, then it's naive to expect and foolish to allow educational elders to assume sole responsibility for defining and delivering *an education*.

Indeed, educators need help to move to the new plateaus which are evolving as a result of seismic societal change. It is a time to envision the education that's beyond the horizon, to build community coalitions, to create systems which enable all Americans to champion children, and to homestead a true learning society.

Are you too busy to think?

Are you too busy to think?

Our business is creating strategic advantage. We help people envision preferred futures and develop plans for getting there. Our clients tend to be ahead of the curve.

Here's why: They understand that thinking is the first step to being a step ahead.

But most people don't have time to think. They're too busy working! Strange, isn't it? How many times have you heard people say that they do their best thinking in the car? But when they pull into the parking lot, they turn off the car and shut down their thinking ... so they can "get to work."

Perhaps that's why there are too few new ideas. Perhaps that's why much of what we do looks like much of what we've already done.

Here's your chance to rebel. Take time to think ... right now. Shut the door. Get comfortable. Read the rest of this section. Then stare out the window. Indulge yourself in 20 minutes of thinking -- 30 if you're radical.

To get started, use *Banach's Woodpecker Questions*. These are questions for which we have an answer, but we're not really sure it's correct. (The classic is: *"Do woodpeckers get headaches?"*)

Scientists tell us that the woodpecker's brain is wrapped in a huge mucous pad, so the bird can bang away all day and never get headaches. So, while the answer to the question is, "No," *we're not really sure.*

Woodpecker Question 1: **Why do we use textbooks?**

> We think we know the answer, but are we really sure? Information is doubling every 18 months -- every 550 days! By the time today's kindergartner moves through the grades to graduation, the body of information will easily be eight times what it is today.

Now, think about this:

> It takes about 10 years to get a textbook to print. From the time the author conceives ideas, develops thoughts, writes the manuscript, edits it, hooks up with a publisher, rewrites the book, and engages in myriad other steps, a decade passes.
>
> Next, a school district curriculum review committee spends two years evaluating the book before making a recommendation (which then passes through the administrative hierarchy before the school board approves it).
>
> Finally, the school district adopts a brand new 12-year old book ... and the students use it for 5 to 7 years, sometimes more.
>
> In this scenario, the student at the end of the line is using a 19-year old book (10 + 2 + 7 = 19).

This leads to a dead duck question: How can a student keep current by reading a 19-year old book? (We have an answer to dead duck questions and we're sure it's right; e.g., Do dead ducks quack?)

Woodpecker Question 2: **Why do schools have to be places?**

> More than a quarter of Americans work at home. Because of the prevalence of technology, the percentage is destined to increase. Many of these home-based workers have computers, fax machines, satellite dishes and sophisticated telephone equipment. Long distance, they look and sound like "real" companies. And who else has access to the technology that makes home-based employment possible? The children of these workers.
>
> So, why should students be transported to a place? They can get their lesson on video, from the best instructors in the world. Why should students spend time in an ill-equipped lab when they can do computer simulations? Why should they write out their lessons long-hand when they can use word processors and fax their lessons to school?

During the 2000's, we will repackage education. Learning will take place in the home, in the community, at school, and even in between. And by the dawning of the new century, we will have dramatic new designs to deliver schooling.

"What about socialization?" asks Brontosaurus Skepticus. "Students won't learn how to interact with one another."

The fact is that there isn't much socializing at school. A lot of kids don't know a lot of other kids. Think about it ... Typically in a high school, there are five or six 55-minute periods with five minutes for passing from one class to the next. How do you socialize when you have to rush from one place to another and be quiet once you get there? (Woodpecker Question 2a!)

Woodpecker Question 3: **Why don't we teach to the test?**

Obviously, it wouldn't be fair ... or so we have learned.

But, if you think about it, education is one of the few arenas where participants often don't know what's expected of them until it's too late.

In every sport, the objective is clear and the evaluation criteria are known before the game begins. Basketball players know they have to get the ball through the hoop more frequently than members of the other team. In baseball, the objective is to score more runs, in football, more points.

In other professions people know the objectives in advance. For example, in medicine, everyone works to heal the patient. In fact, patients are even part of the process. Before any treatment, they know which procedures will be performed, what the expected outcomes are, and their role in the process.

In education the objectives aren't always clear. Most school districts can't tell students and their parents what to expect from a 12-year investment. (Sorry, Brontosaurus Skepticus, we haven't explained what we mean by "a quality education for every child" ... nor have we defined "skills for the changing world of work" or "producing learners who will be fully functioning members of a multi-faceted society.")

Perhaps we should start by spelling out exactly what we want students to learn. Then we should tell them the objectives and expectations up front. We should also make clear their responsibility in the process. Maybe that's all that blocks effective teacher-student-parent partnerships. Maybe that's all that is keeping some students from saying, "Now I understand."

Woodpecker Question 4: **Why can't groups come up with solutions?**

Pick an answer:

(a) They don't have all the data.
(b) There are usually too many people in the group.
(c) Group members don't get along.
(d) None of the above.

The correct answer is d, none of the above.

Groups can't come up with solutions because solutions -- real solutions -- are situational and personal.

Groups are good at identifying issues and obstacles, but they can't accommodate specific situations, local politics, and delicate interrelationships. During group process, people tend to get side-tracked by thinking about how they can survive the problem at home ... or by giving silent thanks that, in the end, it will be Bob or Mary who will have to handle the flak and deal with the fallout.

Good administrators learn from group process, combine new information with what they know, bounce ideas off people at home, and then develop a solution.

This approach does not preclude citizen involvement or building decision-making teams. In fact, wise leaders involve people in things that affect their destiny. But they also realize that groups cannot take responsibility, and that's why a gap often exists between what the group proposes and what works. The person in charge must accommodate the variables and develop localized solutions that have a chance. (This is why we have ring leaders and team captains. Eventually someone has to take responsibility.)

Woodpecker Question 5: **Why are educators so defensive?**

Well, reading scores are down and violence is up; teachers aren't dedicated and administrators don't care. There are all kinds of reasons to be defensive and cover the flanks. But this is a dead duck question with lame duck answers.

The reality is that educators have been assigned both blame and responsibility for society's problems. Most critics follow their list of what's wrong with society (crime, drugs, violence, ill-prepared workers, and so forth) by saying, "The schools have to improve!" (Notice that they don't say that schools reflect society and *we* are society so *we* must improve *our* schools.)

Nothing new here.

America's educational system has taken responsibility in the past. Think about it. The industrial era required workers who were obedient, could handle routine work, didn't have to think too much, and understood the importance of being on time. Look at the ways schools responded. They stressed discipline, drill, and practice, not questioning your elders, and being in your seat ... by the time the bell rings. The public schools produced the workforce that industrial America demanded.

How well did the schools do? (*Dead duck question!*)

American productivity reached new highs. Our quality of life surpassed anything forecasters imagined. U.S. graduate schools enrolled more foreign students than the graduate schools of all other nations combined. And our system of public education was envied throughout the world.

Now we are more than six decades into the Information Age. No one is sure of the future, and hence, there is a lot of finger-pointing -- people seeking to blame someone else for the instability that characterizes their lives. Guess which institution is front and center?

We demand more from our public schools than we do from any other institution (with the possible exception of marriage). And schools have produced what we have demanded.

But now the rules have changed. Knowledge is capital. New alliances have arisen in an international economy. Competition is being redefined, and so is work. We live in turbulent times, and to compensate, we cling to the past and grab for the familiar.

But our new age dictates a renaissance in education as well. Schools must accommodate the change in our society. They must become sensitive to marketplace force -- tailored to customer needs and future-focused. The changes ahead will redefine our concept of school. They will also give us promise for an even better system of public education.

Get involved in the transformation. Start by asking questions. Think about the answers. Share the thoughts. Lead the revitalization wherever you are. Here are some starter questions:

■ Why do teachers have to be people? Okay, why do they have to be people who are trained as teachers?

■ Why do we set up evaluation systems that make students and schools look bad?

■ Why are our schools structured like the factories of the Industrial Age that ended 50 years ago?

■ Why do we spend so much time greasing squeaking wheels while we ignore the things that hum smoothly along?

■ Why is everything bolted onto the curriculum instead of integrated in?

■ Why do we lecture all the time?

Changes come from the questions that we ask. Questions allow us to think, thinking allows us to make connections, connections produce understanding ... and that's what leads to strategic advantage and preferred tomorrows. Before you go back to work, *think about it.*

Change forces and their implications

Change forces and their implications

The context for life itself is being dramatically altered as we move from a period of rapid change to one of *radical* change. The radical changes that we are experiencing and the resultant context that is emerging are both being driven by major demographic shifts, a developing global economy, new coalitions and alliances, and unprecedented advances and discoveries.

In the past we kept up with the accelerating pace of change by running faster and working harder. But these strategies don't always work in a period of radical change because radical change is less linear, more abrupt, and more complex than rapid change.

Radical change generates new rules. It frequently alters "the game" beyond recognition, and often moves the players into new arenas.

As the change forces driving the emerging context become clear and its dimensions become focused, we will see new challenges and opportunities along with new definitions of quality and greatness.

Capitalizing on the opportunities that are presented by these change forces dictates that we think together. Indeed, our ability to understand the forces of change and the caliber of our response to them will most certainly determine the nature of our society and the quality of our future.

To jump-start your thinking, we cite a wide range of change forces on the next few pages. These change forces have been placed in one of nine environmental scanning categories; e.g., *Demographics, Economics, Political Climate*, and so forth. This establishes an organizational frame for the change forces and positions their implications in a tested issues management system.

In each environmental scanning category you'll find two, three, or four change forces. And for each change force you'll find two, three, or four implications.

Understand that there may be a dozen change forces in each environmental scanning category. And each change force might have 50 implications. Who knows?

Here's the point ... and the purpose of this exercise in thinking: If you can add a change force or implication to those we've provided, you're using the change force material just as it was intended -- you're using it to think about the specifics of your situation in the context of a broader perspective.

Environmental Scanning Category: Demographics (vital human statistics)

The future exists today in the form of demographic data. The data tell us about people -- how many there are, where they are, what they're doing, where they are going, and much more. This data can easily be converted into information about tomorrow's students and workers because these future students and workers exist today! Demographic information enables us to think about *what might be* from the perspective of *what is*.

Demographic *Change Force*: The aging of America

Implications

- There will be an increase in the percentage of the population needing care.

- Social, medical, and infrastructure expenditures will increase dramatically.

- More people will alter their exercising and consumption lifestyles.

- "Fountain of youth" products will proliferate.

- Retirement will be redefined as more retirees anticipate drawing pensions longer than they drew paychecks.

- The voter turnout rates of aging Americans will increase.

- Economics will limit entitlements

Demographic *Change Force*: Societal diversity

Implications

∎ Our communities, workplaces, and schools will become increasingly multicultural.

∎ Social causes and special interests will become more diverse, and 50 percent-plus-one majorities will be difficult to attain.

∎ Divergent value systems will emerge and be tested.

∎ Classification of individuals may lead to de facto segregation, and legislation which benefits specific individuals or groups will be amended or repealed.

∎ Diversity may become a liability.

Demographic *Change Force*: Population shifts and dispersion of the citizenry

Implications

∎ There will be stresses on the infrastructure in many suburban and rural areas.

∎ More cities will be incapable of surviving by what they do within their own borders.

∎ There will be little sense of community in satellite communities.

∎ Local politics will be redefined in regions that are populated by people whose economic interests are tied to the global economy.

Environmental Scanning Category: Economics (the workplace, the workforce, and the exchange of value)

All change is first social, then political, and -- finally -- economic. In the end, it seems, everything is driven by economics. Or, as your elders used to say, "Money talks!"

Economics *Change Force*: **Knowledge work**

Implications

- Educational attainment and continuous learning will be significant determinants of an individual's place on the economic continuum.

- More businesses will realize that their competitive advantage is provided primarily by knowledge workers.

- The service sector and the contingency workforce will continue to increase.

- Employers will seek relationships instead of marriages; i.e., workers will be employed not for a lifetime, but to complete an assignment.

- More workers will be alienated and the incidence of workplace violence will increase.

Economics *Change Force*: **The distribution of wealth**

Implications

- Social instability will become more likely as the gap between rich and poor increases.

- The young may resent the old as they pay the higher costs associated with aging.

- The less affluent may unite and learn to use their political clout.

- Significant economic inequities will be reconciled by proactive legislative action or reactive response to civil unrest.

Economics *Change Force*: Unfunded entitlements

<u>Implications</u>

▌ There will be unfulfilled promises and an angry populous.

▌ There will be tax increases and an angry populous.

Environmental Scanning Category:
Political Climate (the governing context in which people and organizations pursue their objectives)

It's a cliche that *all politics is local*. But now there is more of an influence on *all* politics from the local level. And voters easily can learn what their elected representatives have done for them ... today!

Political Climate *Change Force*: Loss of trust

<u>Implications</u>

▌ People will classify to simplify. (Most simplifications are negative; e.g., *big* -- as in bad -- government, *crooked* politicians, *self-centered* business people, *greedy* athletes, etc.)

▌ People are becoming hardened to violations of the public trust. For some people trust has become relative. They believe, for example, that no politician can be trusted, but that some can be trusted more than others.

▌ Trust will no longer be automatic because of one's membership in or affiliation with certain groups. For example, membership in a union does not guarantee trust. Nor does being a medical doctor.

▌ People will become more resistant to change as loss of trust polarizes their viewpoints on a variety of issues.

■ The bases of institutional support will shift as people study and/or seek alternatives.

Political Climate *Change Force*: Populous politics

Implications

■ Local resources and competence may not adequately accommodate shifted responsibility; i.e., local leaders may find themselves "in over their heads."

■ The number of quick fix, simplistic solution regulations will increase.

■ The unintended consequences of political decisions will become more prevalent as decision-makers pursue quick-fix simplicity in a period of complexity.

Political Climate *Change Force*: Politics by poll

Implications

■ Fewer politicians will be *for* anything because one key to electoral success is to be against something.

■ Politicians will follow public opinion more than they will lead their constituents.

■ Those who want political support must learn to build and maintain a public constituency.

Environmental Scanning Category: Social Values & Lifestyles (the beliefs and behaviors of people)

American behavior has been a subject of interest to people around the world since the republic was formed. The future certainly "isn't what it used to be." Neither are our beliefs, values, and behaviors.

Social Values & Lifestyles *Change Force*: **Endangered youth**

Implications

- There will be less support for the education of young people as America ages.

- The "permanent underclass" will grow.

- Feelings of hopelessness will increase among young people.

- The worker and leadership pool will become more shallow.

Social Values & Lifestyles *Change Force*: **Families and households**

Implications

- Diverse family structures will produce children with diverse beliefs, values, and behaviors ... and capacities.

- Parenting failures will produce stresses on schools, churches, and social agencies.

- Schools, churches, and other agencies will be forced to assume more parenting and social development responsibilities.

Social Values & Lifestyles *Change Force*: **Home base**

Implications

- Technology will place the home at the center of a work, consumer, educational, and recreational cloverleaf.

- The reasons that people "go out" will change.

- Businesses will develop to support home base.

- Youngsters with a strong home base will have a tremendous social and economic advantage over those who do not have such support.

Social Values & Lifestyles *Change Force*: The pampered consumer

Implications

- Today's marketplace minimums are quality, speed, convenience, customer service, and price.

- Customer-sensitive organizations will thrive.

- Some customers will expect more than even the most responsible organization can provide.

Social Values & Lifestyles *Change Force*: Incarceration

Implications

- Confinement-related expenditures will continue to escalate.

- The costs of incarceration will have adverse effects on budgets for other social programs and services.

- Economics is beginning to shift concerns from prisoner welfare to victim welfare.

Social Values & Lifestyles *Change Force*: Rights over responsibilities

- The propensity to find fault will intensify.

- It will be even harder "to please everyone."

- People may exercise the right to make decisions before they assume the responsibility to be informed.

- Nuisance lawsuits will increase as people strive to *prove* who's right and who's wrong.

Environmental Scanning Category: Advances & Discoveries (machines, processes, and techniques that enhance or replace people)

Machines are getting cheaper, faster, and smarter. Indeed, advances in processing capacity, software development, networking, photonics, and nanotechnology signal the dawn of thinking machines. While many of our technologies are already way beyond our capacity to use them, now these technologies are being "humanized" so they can help us learn to use them to their full capacity.

Advances & Discoveries *Change Force*: Communication technology

Implications

- Access to information will be global and instantaneous.

- Communication technologies will continue compressing time and space, creating "immediate uncertainties."

- As the number of decisions which need to be made increases, the time available to make them will decrease.

- Cultures and political boundaries will become increasingly irrelevant.

- People will have to master information management skills.

Advances & Discoveries *Change Force*: Human technology

<u>Implications</u>

▌ Artifical organs, genetic research, and cloning will raise ethical and economic questions. (In the end, economic answers will determine courses of action.)

▌ The use of human technologies will be driven by attempts to alter and prevent disabilities ... and to gain human advantage.

▌ There will be a need to reassess entitlements, pensions, and social programs which were not designed to accommodate long lives.

Advances & Discoveries *Change Force*: Mechatronics

<u>Implications</u>

▌ Scientists will continue to produce smarter machines.

▌ People will become more reliant on and trusting of machines.

▌ There may be a need to dummy down workers.

Advances & Discoveries *Change Force*: Nanotechnology

<u>Implications</u>

▌ Medical diagnosis and treatment will be revolutionized

▌ There will be new paradigms for manufacturing.

▌ "Raw material" will be redefined (and the supply of many natural resources will be less consequential).

▌ Learning will take on new dimensions. (A 1/200th-inch "nanocube" could contain all the world's books!)

Environmental Scanning Category:
Education (society's efforts to produce
an enlightened citizenry)

Education is being redefined, and the driving forces are entrepreneurs, technology ... and learners. While school people look at new ways to do old things and use technology to do the same things faster, private enterprise and the people it serves have moved beyond the creation of data and information to the expansion of knowledge.   As schools are pulled in this direction, success will come to those that focus on the needs of learners, giving them what they need when they need it. And while the new technologies can equalize opportunities for learning, the work environment these technologies produce will *not* be an equal opportunity employer.

Education *Change Force*: Digital learning materials

Implications

- Access to information will be universal.

- The marketplace will drive "universal" languages.

- Information storage and delivery will be redefined.

- It will be easier to create and share knowledge.

Education *Change Force*: Distance learning

Implications

- Technology will expand the number of educational options because people will be able to learn anything, anywhere, anytime ... with transparent technology.

- The quality of instructional materials will improve.

- Instruction will increasingly be "packaged" for consumption at the convenience of the learner

- Educational institutions and educational roles will be redefined.

Education *Change Force*: Legislated standards

Implications

- ∎ Legislative initiatives will not be systemic and, hence, will not be sustainable.

- ∎ The focus of education will shift from learning to compliance (and from compliance to "creative compliance").

- ∎ Educators may be the first group of professionals to be divested of their profession.

Education *Change Force*: Privatization

Implications

- ∎ As the founding principles of America's public education system are lost in the privatization movement, the less able and the disadvantaged will be affected first.

- ∎ Educators will dissipate energy resisting privatization instead of looking for the partnering opportunities.

- ∎ The well being of the learner may become secondary to the economics of the learning process.

Environmental Scanning Category: Public Opinion (commonly held perceptions and understandings)

The ultimate court is the court of public opinion. Nothing can survive without its support; nothing can make headway against its current.

Public Opinion *Change Force*: Public opinion paradox

Implications

- More solutions to problems will find simultaneous favor and disfavor.

- Leaders will be forced to focus on the development of critical masses.

- Good will and eternal gratitude will be temporary possessions.

Public Opinion *Change Force*: Alienation

Implications

- Leaders will need a contingency plan for every decision.

- The "get even" electorate will continue to evolve.

- Attitudes about term limits, anti-incumbency, and fringe alternatives to governance will intensify.

Public Opinion *Change Force*: Fear of crime

Implications

- Anyone hoping to attract a customer must create an environment which is safe *and* is perceived to be safe.

- Support for concealed weapons legislation will increase.

- Quick-fix legislation designed to prevent crime and punish criminals will be approved with little regard the cost of physical facilities necessary for incarceration and even less regard for the related operating expenses.

Environmental Scanning Category:
Organizational Context (how people organize to relate, share, achieve, and compete)

People are organizing to relate, share, achieve, and compete by going it alone and going it together, *simultaneously*. While businesses form partnerships with one another so they can create strategic advantage together, they are downsizing at the middle management and professional levels. This downsizing, in turn, allows entrepreneurs to go it alone, using their knowledge to develop new enterprises.

Organizational Context *Change Force*: Changing size

Implications

- Productivity gains may be offset by fallout from employee layoffs.

- Employee loyalty will dissipate as companies show little regard for the individuals in their workforce.

- Customer loyalty will dissipate as most consumers become lost in the confusion surrounding growth, mergers, and downsizing.

- Stresses on workers and organizational systems will increase.

Organizational Context *Change Force*: Boundary breaking

Implications

- Geographic, political, and even organizational boundaries will become increasingly meaningless in the digital age.

- More workers and organizations will be linked in electronic (virtual) partnerships.

- Vision and leadership will be critical guides to employees and organizations that are loosely structured.

Organizational Context *Change Force*: Partnering

<u>Implications</u>

- Organizations will identify their core competencies and use them to broker collaborative ventures.

- Organizations will form partnerships within and beyond their communities.

- People within organizations will need to define the value they add and the strategic advantage they bring to the partnership.

Organizational Context *Change Force*: Growth of entrepreneurs

<u>Implications</u>

- In the digital age marked by radical change, the niche markets will belong to the entrepreneurs.

- The amount of work outsourced and the number of contingency workers will be driven by entrepreneurs.

- Entrepreneurs will form alliances with consumers.

- Marketplace-sensitive organizations will flourish.

Environmental Scanning Category:
World Affairs (interactions of groups and nations that affect the marketplace or political climate)

New coalitions are forming, new economic entities are being defined, and new political alliances are changing historical perspectives. Indeed, the capacity to create change has become global in scope.

World Affairs *Change Force*: Globalization

Implications

- The domination of world economic and political events will change.

- Different cultures will have to create shared values for a common world.

- The global economy will define the power of nations, and determine the nature of work and the quality of life everywhere.

World Affairs *Change Force*: Lack of geopolitical structure

Implications

- Isolationism will be the victim of global economics.

- Entire societies will face the implications of radical change and the emerging global economy.

- Leaders must focus on the development of compatible visions.

In each of the environmental scanning categories, it's increasingly apparent that external forces trigger most change. Things that happen outside the boundaries of our organizations, institutions, and personal lives now exert a greater influence over how we do business, what we believe, and how we behave. Yet, in this environment of externally activated change, it's paradoxical that opportunities (and crises) are frequently created by our internal systems -- organizational, institutional, and personal.

Capitalizing on change requires us to open rather than to close these internal systems to the new global context. We must question not only what we do, but why and how we do it. We must realize that using a bigger hammer is not always an appropriate strategy, and we must admit that in a changing context we don't have all the answers, that we need to rethink some of our approaches, that we need to think beyond our tested solutions, and that we need to take intelligent, creative, and bold risks.

Overcoming resistance to change

Overcoming resistance to change

Change is good. -- tennis star Andre Agassi after his shoulder-length hair was turned into a buzz.

Today, the teacher who works for or allows the status quo is the traitor ... personal purpose is the route to organizational change. -- Michael Fullan

These might be the words of any school teacher or administrator. For decades, observers of education have been calling for improvement, for different approaches to learning, for change.

In the 1960s educators tried new delivery systems for classroom lessons, but the results were questionable. Then a crisis in confidence developed in the 1970s, and people began to question whether the educational establishment was capable of change.

The early 1980s saw a plethora of suggestions for reform, including the widely cited report, *A Nation at Risk.* More recently, educators have focused on reform and restructuring, but the action that leads to systemic change is still lacking.

Has the public waited too long? Will people give up on the education establishment and take action themselves? The increase in home schooling, the call for vouchers and schools of choice, and increased influence of outside political groups indicate that this may be the case.

Can educators change schools to meet the evolving needs of students? The jury is clearly still out.

Let's look at change in high schools

Those who contend that true educational reform won't happen point their fingers at one segment of the K-12 education community -- high schools. A commonly held perception is that secondary school educators are far more resistive to change than they should be or than their elementary peers are.

Is perception fact or fiction? Debating how many high school educators go into spasms when people talk about choice adds little to the improvement of education. The mere fact that any educator who refuses to look at new ways to work with students tells us that learners are not being served as well as they might be. The facts are: the world is changing, students must be prepared for a world we can't describe, and schools have a major responsibility for that preparation.

Our challenge is to understand why some educators refuse to acknowledge change and to nurture those who do.

We know that many high school educators are open to change, and, in fact, are consistently looking for ways to improve the school climate or to make today's lessons more meaningful than last year's. However, there are others -- too many in a society of change -- who believe what worked five years ago is just as likely to work next year. Those are the attitudes that must be changed if our schools are to be competitive.

How we train and organize our teachers

Elementary teachers are trained to teach a variety of subjects, and the subject matter is related to the growth and development of children. Elementary teachers are concerned with what is "developmentally appropriate." Some say their collegiate training prepares them to teach children. Whatever the reasons, elementary teachers seem most willing to change and try new things.

Junior high school educators seemed to be in a no-man's land between elementary school and high school. Here the instructional focus begans to shift from the whole child to specific content areas. This shift in focus seems to parallel a growing resistance to change. However, the movement from the junior high to middle school concept has brought more teaming to the schools serving our adolescents. This, in turn, has produced multi-discip- linary teams and a spirit of working together for the well being of the student. Perhaps the training for teaming, by itself, has increased the willingness of middle level teachers to change.

High school teachers still spend the majority of their collegiate careers focused on a content area. For example, they are prepared to teach English or history or math or science. And, in many areas of specialization, much of the content doesn't change. High school teachers might then ask, "If the content doesn't change, why should we?"

In addition to the specifics of the secondary school environment, much that all teachers confront flies in the face of encouraging change. Professional development is one example. There is never enough. And, as budgetary concerns become pronounced, one of the first cuts is professional training.

Simple logic tells us that people are unlikely to change if they are not exposed frequently and continuously to new ideas. Yet, many school systems require educators to cover their own expenses when they travel to a professional meeting. Some school districts refuse to pay for substitute time when teachers want to attend a professional event. Even memberships in professional organizations too often have to be personally financed.

When professional development eventually is provided to teachers, its very structure questions whether it promotes true change. For instance, often consultants are brought into a school system for a 3-hour session on a certain topic. They deliver their presentation and leave. There's no follow-up. There's no attempt to focus segments of training to reach a change objective.

The same pattern follows with much of the training that professional organizations provide. Typically, a convention or seminar consists of numerous unrelated sessions that provide a potpourri of speakers but no process for systemic change.

Guidelines to change

A key assumption for effective reform is that change is a process, not an event. Yet, too much of an educator's professional development is a series of unrelated events. With event-oriented training, educators have difficulty implementing new ideas, let alone instituting systemic reform.

The National Staff Development Council tells us that ... *professional development plans too often ignore general principals of adult learning. Five guidelines regarding the process of individual change should be considered.*

The Council cites these guidelines:

1. Adult learning experiences must be based on research and proven practice.

2. Effective staff development must foster educators' confidence in their ability to be successful on the job.

3. Successful professional development must increase both independence and collaboration.

4. Identifying staff development outcomes is imperative.

5. Successful designs for learning require time, resources, and supporting structures.

If educators are serious about providing professional development that will lead to effective, long-term change, they must pay attention to these guidelines, especially the last two. They must move past the hit-and-miss, now-and-then mentality.

How we introduce teachers to teaching

What may have an even more negative impact on change for teachers is how they are introduced to the profession. Initial training comes during college days when they too frequently are taught by university professors who have been away from elementary and high school classrooms for a long time. Some introduce budding teachers to antiquated ideas right from the start.

As prospective teachers move through the college experience, they become student teachers. Often they see professionals teaching in a passive mode that has been practiced in too many schools for too long. Too often they watch students who are not involved in, let along responsible for, their own learning. And, when these young graduates move to their own classroom, they emulate what they've experienced. As people are taught, so do they teach.

While these conditions and circumstances inhibit willingness to change, clearly they do not prohibit it. An environment that is conducive and supportive to taking risks enables many teachers to try new ideas and strategies. Yet, something else is developing that discourages change even more -- the trend toward public involvement in schools.

Responding to public pressure

Educators are now faced with more public pressure than ever before -- pressure from parents, government leaders, the business community, and the news media. The involvement of these groups can be positive, and, in fact, can stimulate change.

Today, however, too much involvement is accompanied by finger-pointing. Many groups come to school board meetings or school site council meetings to promote single-issue agendas. The net effect is the creation of additional roadblocks to change. Educators ask why they should embrace different ideas if they are likely to be publicly attacked. Community discord related to outcome-based education was certainly one example of this.

How to introduce change

How then do we move change into the vocabulary of educators, especially secondary school educators?

Appropriate, consistent professional development is a major start. But school boards and others must be willing to make the financial investment in training that will bring about change.

Training must ...

- be focused on specific objectives;
- be systematic in nature; and,
- allow teachers to see that change can help their performance.

The National Association of Secondary School Principals believes that anti-change attitudes are dissipating:

> *The more that reform is discussed, the more informed people become about change. The more positive experiences teachers and others have with change; the more change we will see. Teachers who have experienced how exciting reform is don't want to return to the old ways.*

Also, if proactive change is going to become a constant in American education, those who are in leadership roles will have to communicate that purposeful experimentation and intelligent risk-taking is okay -- in fact, necessary.

If school boards, superintendents, and principals don't encourage change, then few teachers will take the risk. Leaders must clearly communicate that it's okay to stumble if you are trying to implement strategies that will benefit learners.

While we can do much to promote change in the education establishment, we must also pay attention to the public arena. Few of us like to be unfairly criticized, and public criticism comes frequently when new ideas are introduced in public education. Sometimes the criticism comes in public meetings, but frequently it's through the news media. When a new idea is tried, it can frequently be evaluated on radio and television talk shows, in the letters to the editors column, or in editorials or op-ed articles before it ever has a chance to succeed. Educators ask, *"Why try something new when we are tried in the court of public opinion before the reform even has a chance to succeed?"*

To complicate matters even more, educators typically receive little or no training in media relations and other public relations skills. Frequently they are forced to do battle on a battlefield they don't comprehend. Teachers and school administrators must understand that change requires public support, and support is built through effective communication.

To make reform less painful and to become change agents, educators at all levels must become more efficient in public relations. The first requirement is simply to understand that public communication is not a frill or a diversion for educators, but an investment in success. If external audiences -- parents, business people, community leaders, legislators, government officials -- understand and support change, reform is much more likely to succeed.

While a comprehensive public relations effort is required to give any reform effort a chance of success, most educators think public relations means "getting more good news in the newspapers."

Educators must become more strategic in media relations. Pat Ordovensky, former education writer for *USA TODAY*, says there are two times when educators and journalists come together. "The first is when we (reporters) want something from you, and the second is when you want something from us."

Educators shouldn't avoid going to the news media. They should adopt a page from the strategy books of politicians who plan ways to communicate their messages to the public through the news media and practice ways to implement that strategy.

Here are some suggestions for improving your media relations:

- Identify the reporters who are likely to cover your schools.

- Understand that education is not an easy beat, and that education reporters turn over frequently. Both factors can lead to inaccurate coverage.

- The more you can do to inform reporters, the more accurate their stories will be. Reporters appreciate your attention.

- Treat all reporters equally. Don't give briefings to only half of the reporters who cover your schools, or don't brief four reporters on Friday and five the following Wednesday.

- If newspapers in your area are likely to take an editorial stance on an educational change, ask for a meeting with the editorial board or the editor of the newspaper. Present the change and the rationale for it so that the editors know *your* view before they determine their position.

- Ask editors for editorial support.

- Many newspapers -- large and small -- publish op-ed pieces, those articles on the editorial pages expressing opinion and written by people who aren't on the newspaper staff. Consider writing or encouraging respected citizens in yourcommunity to write an op-ed article presenting your views onreform. During a hotly contested issue, you may well find your opponents' names on such an article. Beat them to the punch.

- Consider taking your message to legitimate talk shows on radio and television stations in your community. But before you make that decision, listen to the show and determine the audience.

Get a feel for the type of questions that are generally asked. If you believe that the show provides a legitimate opportunity to present your views, consider it.

The educational enterprise must learn to embrace change. It isn't something to be feared; rather, it's another tool to be used on our journey toward the future. Michael Fullan identifies four "core capacities" each of us needs to develop to build greater change capacity. He calls them *personal vision-building* (creating our own positive images as driving forces), *inquiry* (keeping current by persistent questioning), *mastery* (learning to be competent and current), and *collaboration* (working with others to accomplish things).

Ten lies we keep telling ourselves

Ten lies we keep telling ourselves

Computers now exhibit the rudiments of human intelligence. Money and information are moved around the globe electronically, crossing geographic and political boundaries in nanoseconds. Ahead are the dividends of research into superconductivity, biogenetics, and planetary engineering.

Indeed, the context for life itself is being dramatically altered as we move from a period of rapid change. In such a world, you can't keep up by running faster.

Today, running faster is often a strategy of diminishing returns -- so is working harder. As this new context for life evolves, it will create new definitions of quality and greatness:

- world-class standards will emerge;
- mediocrity and minimums will disappear as benchmarks; and,
- increasingly, we will find ourselves faced with issues that are beyond our experience, tested strategies, and knowledge.

Yet, great numbers of people ignore this radical change and the emerging context that it is creating. Many advocate a return to more comfortable times. Some try other means of escape, hoping that things will be better when they tune back in.

But efforts to deny and resist radical change produce a sense of security that is founded on falsehoods. In this womb of self-deception, here are the top ten lies that people tell themselves:

1. *Schools are not businesses.* They may not be like other businesses, but they are businesses. In fact, schools are often the biggest economic enterprise in town. Believing (and then acting) like a non-business is the first step to making the non-business lie become a self-fulfilling prophecy. While public opinion is clear on the virtues of an educated citizenry, people are uncertain about the best way to attain this objective. They are searching for new ideas and strategies.

This heightened consumer interest in the quality of schooling is altering perceptions and changing education's market environment. As people think about new options for learning, they inevitably generate competition in the educational arena. Choice legislation is just one option that can potentially knock some of the players out of the game. In fact, large numbers of people are banking on it.

2. *This too shall pass.* Au contraire, this too shall *not* pass. The speed of change will not slow. The geometric growth of information will not stop. The consequences of the emerging context will not go away.

We are unfamiliar with continuous radical change, and we have not had to deal with the waves of contextual transformation that it produces. For example, we have not had to deal with the de-massification of society, minority majorities, smart homes, and instructional consumerism -- all at the same time! We have not had to accommodate the speed of satellite communication, the powerful learning potential that is provided by computer disks, and the synergy that is produced by global interrelationships.

The emerging context is generating new energy with every change that it produces. Count on things to accelerate. Look for new knowledge, new ideas, and new opportunities for the caliber of life to spiral upward. Radical change such as this cannot be accommodated by "waiting it out."

3. *Local control is a blessing.* It's a blessing and a curse. Our system of local control controls less with every passing day. Just as a nation divided is destined to fall, so too may our educational system. Sixteen thousand individual school boards may be close to the people, but independently they can't develop a collective comprehension of radical change and identify the consequences of the emerging context. Even if they did, they'd find it difficult to develop a common vision and customer-oriented strategic response.

While the global need is for interdependence and cooperation, local control fosters isolation and competition. In the emerging context, radical change is frequently subtracting positive points from local control's plus-minus list.

4. *There must have been a communication breakdown.* Communication has been a scapegoat too long. It's the system or the process that breaks down, not communication. When vision, mission, and goals are unclear, it's not the result of a communication breakdown. It's the result of somebody dropping the ball. When we fail to take a risk or pursue an opportunity, ineptness might be better attributed to organizational culture or climate than communication.

   When communication breaks down -- if it does! -- it gets better. The grapevine expands to handle more volume. New grapevines emerge. Informal communication increases, and special newsletters and memoranda are disseminated. Communication rarely "breaks down."

5. *There isn't enough time.* While we are busier by the day, we do find time for the people and things we value. If it's important to us, there's always enough time.

   But a half-truth is embedded in this lie. If we try to make our schools all things to all people, it's quite likely that we won't have enough time (or enough resources or enough energy!).

   We must learn to invest our time more wisely. We can do so by making some fundamental changes in how we conduct our business. For instance,

   - we can ask why we have some of the meetings we do;
   - we can restructure those meetings that are necessary to generate open and honest dialogue;
   - we can realize that talking consumes the same amount of time as acting;
   - we can tie incentives and rewards to performance outcomes; and,
   - we can make our limited time more productive by spending it with high-energy people. (*See Lie #8.*)

6. *Staff training is a luxury.* This is a knowledge-based society, and educators are in the knowledge business. The more our knowledge becomes obsolete, the more we do a disservice to learners -- not to mention the educational profession.

The emerging context demands continuous learning. What's more, it dictates that educational inservice programs move beyond the status quo to generate an awareness of change, to elevate individual and collective agendas, and to create the visions and systems that will help learners of all aspirations and abilities. Active participation in training is a commitment that all educators must make. Every winning team from sports to medicine to the military is characterized by learning and practice -- *regular* learning and practice. We should demand no less for and from the instructional team. Finding baby-sitters so that educators can increase their capacity is an inconvenience that parents should celebrate.

7. *The resource pit has no bottom.* Every organization faces demands that exceed its resources. When all the demands are accommodated, the result is over-commitment. This is painfully obvious at both the state and national levels where deficit details clearly indicate that government coffers have been extended beyond their supporting resources.

Belief in the bottomless pit has placed many institutions -- both public and private -- on a curve that is destined to collide with revenue realities. Whether the cause is unclear vision, lousy management, or crooked king pins, the result is always bounced checks or unfulfilled promises.

Over-expenditures are also destined to collide with skeptical consumers and overburdened taxpayers. Unfulfilled promises are not going down easily these days, and more people are expressing their disgust with governmental excesses. Pushed beyond their limits, these are the people who ultimately will say, "That's it ... we've had enough!"

The people pool also has a bottom. "You can be replaced!" is an old truism that may become a new resource-related lie. Today there are shortages of workers who can handle the knowledge jobs that are proliferating in our workplace. As a result of a demographically driven shortage and the education and training investment required to develop sophisticated skills, many of today's workers may not be replaceable. At the very least, the personnel talent pool is not as deep as it used to be.

8. *One person cannot make a difference.* Great lie! One person with a vision, enough knowledge to take the first step, and a few guts *can* make a difference. Two of these people together generate electricity!

   Management's great challenge is to develop processes that allow us to support the electric people who make a difference, instead of the small number of squeaking wheels who now consume the great bulk of our time. (*See Lie #5.*)

   Watch for organizational leaders to sanction special teams, task forces, "skunk works," and a variety of other organizational forms in an effort to circumvent the slowness, the resistance to change, and the creativity-inhibiting characteristics of bureaucracy. While this may cause some sparks and bruised egos, the new approaches will make it increasingly easy for one person to get the job done.

9. *Don't ask me why; it's the rule.* Sometimes this lie is disguised, but you can spot it if you listen for sentences that begin with these words: "*They* said ... " or "*They* make us ..." or "Now *they're* telling us to ..."

   Customer indifference causes people to quit doing business with a business. While it can occur anywhere in an organization, it does the most damage at the outposts of the system. That's where people contact is the most personal. Most customers don't stop visiting a store (or flying on a particular airline or getting a car serviced at a certain dealership) because they were offended by the president or an organizational chieftain. They leave because they feel someone at the boundary of the system -- for example, a clerk, a nurse, a secretary, a technician, a teacher -- didn't treat them well or didn't care. So they take their business elsewhere.

Education's clients are not addressing their questions to some amorphous *they*. They are asking *you*. To them, you are the boss; you are *they*. If you don't provide an answer, guidance, or a sympathetic ear, they'll think less of you and all your organization represents. (*See Lie #1*.) Indifference is the best way to lose a customer. Hiding behind they, them, the management, or the rule is one of the first symptoms of this customer-killing disease.

10. *We're the professionals (...and we know what's best).* Almost every profession has created partnerships with people. Lawyers, accountants, and consultants work with their clients (customers!). The medical profession actually makes the patient (customer) part of the process. The more professionals know what's best, the less likely they are to take sole responsibility for it.

   Smart professionals don't have all the answers. They seek all the help they can get, and they've learned that things always work better when people work together. Educational professionals who are positive that they know what's best won't ever have "quality parent participation" or "meaningful citizen involvement."

These ten lies are symptoms of self-deception. People use them to deny what has been and to hide from the reality of what is. They also blind us to what can be. If you're telling these lies, be aware. If you're believing them, seek help.

What people choose when they have a choice

What people choose when they have a choice

What influences the choices people make? Perhaps they see "the grass as greener" somewhere else. Or, perhaps, they're dissatisfied with a product, a program, a service, or a person, and have decided to exercise other options. Sometimes they simply want to try something different. There are myriad reasons to exercise a choice.

And each of the reasons can have complicating factors. For example, in truth, the grass may be greener on the other side. Or it may be perceived to be greener. Or people simply may believe it must be greener because they know it's brown where they are.

Personal values drive all behavior all the time. People do what they do because whatever they do satisfies some personal need that they have. And this is what makes human behavior difficult to understand and predict.

We know, for example, that quality, speed, convenience, customer service, and price are driving values for the American consumer. We also know that one or more of these values may be more important to some people than they are to others.

For example, some people don't care about price if they receive quality. They believe that "you get what you pay for." Other people care about both price and quality -- they want "a good bang for the buck." Then there are those who care only about price. Sometimes they'll spend an afternoon driving halfway across town to save 50 cents.

On some occasions all five values drive a decision, which is why you occasionally buy milk at the party store on the way home. While the price is usually higher, you believe that the quality of the milk is the same as in a supermarket. Given this, you choose to make your purchase at the party store because you're in a hurry to get home, you know that you can park by the door, and that you can make your purchase without running to the back of the store. You also know you won't have to wait in a long line behind someone who is stocking up for the 100-year floods.

The five driving values -- quality, speed, convenience, customer service, and price -- also affect the lens through which people view schools. Take parents, for example. They are one of education's most important customers. In most cases, they determine where they will live and which school district their children will attend. And, if they can determine which school building their child will attend, they make that choice, too.

How parents make this choice should be of fundamental importance to educators. Let's look at some of the influences on parents, and think about how these environmental factors might shape perceptions and behavior and influence the choice decision.

First, it's important to remember that a variety of forces influence the decisions parents make. For example, if the local newspaper has been on a year-long campaign to prove that Johnny can't read, the newspaper can have an influence on the decisions parents will make (assuming people read the newspaper and believe it). Similarly, if politicians are on the campaign trail talking about the sorry state of public school graduates, they have potential for affecting people's beliefs, and -- ultimately -- their perspectives, opinions, and behaviors.

Obviously, it's important for school marketers to know what kinds of information people are getting from which sources. It's also important to know what people believe about their schools.

Opinions and choice

When researchers assess organizational image, they often find that the attitudes of employees have a significant influence on what people think about the organization. For example, in the private sector pollsters have discovered that more than two-thirds of respondents who quit doing business with a business say the reason was a negative contact with an employee of that business. Typically, the negative contact occurs where there is an opportunity for customer contact; for example, at the service desk in a store or at the checkout counter in the supermarket. When people in these customer-contact positions don't smile or are indifferent to customers or don't appear interested in helping or carry on a conversation with co-workers while ignoring a customer, the impressions are negative.

These negatives block the building of a business-customer relationship. Odds are the customer won't return. Worse yet, odds are very good the customer will tell 7-10 other people about his negative experience. And, if the business-customer encounter results in rudeness or some other ill-mannered behavior by an employee, the game's over. The customer is unlikely to ever return unless there's some monumental -- and usually expensive! -- "reconcile and recover-" initiative.

This is why business people keep saying that they don't want any negative contacts. They result in lost customers, and that's a cost business can't afford. The same is true for schools.

You can assess how well your organization is interfacing with customers by using the "Points of contact-" form in Exhibit B. This form can be used to evaluate a school district or to assess the quality of an individual's customer contacts. Simply list all the points at which customers (or publics) interface with the system (or a school or a classroom or an individual). Then use whatever criteria you want to assign an A, B, C, D, or FAIL grade to that point of contact. And then identify one or more ways to make a significant improvement in that point of contact. For example, one point of contact may be the voice mail system. All things considered, we might give the voice mail system a grade of C. And we might determine that it could be significantly improved if the recorded voice were more pleasing and the system allowed callers the option of speaking with a human. (See Appendix C.)

EXHIBIT B

Points of Contact

Point of contact	A, B, C, D, FAIL	A significant improvement
Voice mail system	C	Improve greeting Assure access to a human
_____	___	_____
_____	___	_____
_____	___	_____

What people want from their schools

A host of organizations -- private and public, for-profit and not-for-profit -- have researched what people want from their schools. In effect, these organizations sought to determine what people would look for in a school if they could choose. All of the studies produced general agreement. People prefer schools with:

■ high standards and expectations;

■ a safe and caring learning environment;

■ an educational program that prepares students for success in the world of work and in life in general;

■ a customer-friendly atmosphere which values and encourages parental involvement in the school program;

■ well-trained educators and support staff who put children first; and,

■ a sufficient financial base to provide the programs and services people need and want.

Research conducted under the auspices of the Evaluation Center at Western Michigan University focused on school reporting system. Interviewers asked parents what kinds of information they wanted about their child's school. The study included hundreds of parents from across America, and generated the following rank order:

■ information about school safety and parent and community involvement;

■ information about programs available, particularly special offerings such as gifted/talented programming, programs for the students with problems, magnet schools, special education programming, and so forth;

- information about staffing and teacher characteristics; e.g., pupil-teacher ratios, number of teachers with advanced degrees, and so forth;

- standardized testing information;

- student engagement information;

- school success information such as accreditation status;

- quality of school facilities;

- services available to students;

- background information on students; and,

- school finances.

Interestingly, when school superintendents were asked what kinds of information parents wanted, they reversed the rank order established by parents; i.e., superintendents said parents wanted school finance information more than anything else. The superintendents said parents would be least interested in information about student safety and parent-community involvement.

A survey of Michigan households provides additional insights into the beliefs and values of people. More than 1,300 adults across Michigan were asked questions related to school choice. While the responses can't be generalized to others states and communities with any degree of confidence, the findings should provide insights to those who are planning educational marketing programs.

Getting right to the point, Michigan interviewers asked parents: "Suppose, at public expense, you could send your child to any school you wanted -- public, private, or parochial. Would you take your child out of the school he or she now attends?" Nearly two-thirds (63%) of the parents said they would not remove their child.

Those parents who said that they would not remove their children were then asked: "What's the main reason you would leave your child in the school he or she now attends?" More than half (51%) of the respondents said that they would leave their child in his/her current school because they liked the school program and the quality of instruction. The second most frequent response related to the quality of the staff.

Responses to these questions indicate that a substantial majority of parents are satisfied with their youngsters' schools, and that the main reasons are the quality of the program and staff.

If parents like the current school program, what are the elements of the program that generate favorable impressions. To get at this subject, the Michigan pollsters asked this question: "People say it is important for students to have a good education. What comes to mind when you think about a good education?" When the answers were tabulated, there was little difference between the most frequent responses from the total sample and the parent subset, as follows:

Response	Total	Parents
Quality instruction in the basics	25%	23%
Quality of teachers/staff	22	26
Students prepared for work	15	12
Diversity of programs and services	10	10
Test scores	6	5

Even a cursory look at the findings indicates that one of the driving consumer values -- quality -- is high on the list of things people want from their schools. Those engaged in marketing schools would be wise to tell people about the competence and dedication of the school staff, and the caliber of instruction in the basics. In fact, good marketers use this as the point of departure for talking about other school programs and services.

What about the world of work -- what do people mean when they say students should be prepared for the world of work? Again, the Michigan survey provides insight. Respondents were asked this question: "Some people say schools should prepare students for the world of work. What kinds of skills do you think students need to be prepared for the world of work?" Here are the most frequent responses:

Response	Total
Basic skills	28%
Using technology	18
Personal qualities	12
Using information	10
Applying technology	8

The sample survey instrument in *Appendix B* contains questions which will help you determine how people define various components of the educational process, what they like and dislike about their schools, their priorities, and other factors which affect their choices. You are encouraged to amend the sample survey instrument to assess public opinions in your community.

Why people choose charters

While there are now hundreds of charter schools across the country, there is limited data on whether or not they're improving student achievement..

The U.S. Department of Education has commissioned a an annual survey of all charter schools (with follow-up studies and visitations to selected schools.)

This research project has resulted in several findings of particular interest to educational marketers. In addition to providing a profile of charter schools, researchers sought to determine the reasons for founding a charter school. As the following display indicates, "to realize a vision" was the number one response. However, it's interesting to note that this response was mentioned by less than one-third of the "pre-existing public" school charters. The driving reason for their founding was "autonomy."

Here are the totals and the responses from various subsets of the sample (newly created charters, pre-existing public school charters, and pre-existing private school charters):

Most important reason for founding charter school	Total	Newly created	Pre-existing public	Pre-existing private
Realize a vision	51%	67%	28%	35%
Autonomy	21	8	50	--
Special population	13	20	3	5
Financial reasons	6	1	10	20
Parent involvement	5	4	6	5
Attract students	5	1	3	35

Readers can keep abreast of the latest findings in this longitudinal research study by logging on to http://www.ed.gov/offices/OERI/GFI/gfichart.html.

When it comes to why parents choose charter schools, researchers at the conservative Hoover Institute have reported that parents say that their choice was based on: the small size of the school (53%); higher standards (46%); the educational philosophy (44%); more parental involvement (43%); and, better teachers (42%).

Parents of charter school students queried by the Hoover Institute identified a variety of reasons that they were satisfied with their child's school. Note that the list contains reasons that people could give for attending any school. For example, a parent could say that he sends his child to a public (or private or parochial) school because of class size, parent participation, the standards, or the quality of teaching. A marketing person might ask these questions about the following list: Is there anything on the list that we can or can't provide? Is the quality (speed, convenience, price) better than what we provide? Are the items on this list a reflection of fact or perception?

In the competitive educational marketplace, questions like this can help us improve the quality of our programs and attend to public perceptions of them. As you read the list below, ask what's here that your school doesn't, can't or won't provide.

- Parent participation opportunities
- Class size
- Curriculum
- School size
- Individual attention by teachers
- Academic standards
- Accessibility and openness
- Parent expectations for the school
- The people running the school
- The quality of teaching

The bottom line on choice

Educational choice is a reality in most states. More states will certainly hop on the wagon because providing people with a choice generates politically powerful rhetoric. After all, freedom of choice is the American way.

Yet, while many public school administrators are wringing their collective hands in regard to choice, initial studies reveal little, if any, improvement in student achievement as a result of choice programs. In fact, the common denominator in most choice programs is that people tend to choose schools that are just like them -- socially, racially, and economically.

In addition, there is little evidence to indicate that parents make informed decisions about academics when they choose their child's school. This led one Harvard University researcher to conclude that unregulated choice programs unfairly discriminate against parents who are not "savvy educational consumers."

Certainly the future will present a multitude of studies which point out the pros and cons of choice and various educational alternatives such as charters, distance learning, and virtual schools.

In the end, however, the pro and con research may simply fuel a lively debate which, we believe, will result in across-the-board choice and funding which supports a variety of educational alternatives. This means that it will be really unusual for public schools to be doing business as usual.

Public schools probably offer more educational choices than any educational institution. It's apparent, from a marketing point of view, that educators need to help people understand what they do, how good they are at what they do, and engage their communities in the educational process.

We know what people like and dislike. We know what they think and believe. And, while choice is ultimately a personal decision based on personal values, we have the information we need to design marketing programs which will help assure that public schools receive full consideration when people make their choices.

In the future public schools will be just one of the options on the educational smorgasbord. Ironically, this means that public schools will need to make a fundamental choice of their own: should they provide and market the choices that people want, or should they allow others to capture a larger share of the changing educational marketplace.

The ABCs of planning and marketing
An outline

The ABCs of planning and marketing
An outline

You are ready to begin using The Market-Driven System® for planning and marketing if you ...

- ▮ understand that planning and marketing are processes, not one-time events;

- ▮ are prepared to commit resources to the process;

- ▮ want to move quickly from planning to doing;

- ▮ want to be sensitive to your customers' needs and wants;

- ▮ want a process which enables your school district to continually accommodate changing environmental conditions;

- ▮ want to involve people in shaping their future; and,

- ▮ are ready to champion the process.

The Market-Driven System® (The MDS) combines strategic planning and marketing into a single process which can be implemented at the district and building levels. The process can help you capitalize on the change initiatives already underway in your schools. In fact, The MDS can serve as an umbrella under which all such activities can be coordinated.

The MDS process helps you involve people at all levels. It provides a systemic approach to change. It pushes people beyond site-based decision-making to site-based responsibility. And, it can help you make something happen fast. (Most districts can have a written plan and marketing program in place within three months!)

The MDS is a "top-down, bubble-up" process. In the process, vision and mission come from the top. At the district level it's the school board and superintendent who determine where the district is headed.

Of course, determining district direction isn't done in a vacuum. District leaders base their vision on marketplace intelligence (*analysis!*). They determine the district's vision and misson after conducting opinion polls of staff and community, after town meetings or listening forums of some kind, after studying school district demographics, and after analyzing the implications of continuous change.

All this analytical information is shared with key stakeholders, and provides a frame for staff planning. In effect, the vision and mission established by the school board and superintendent provide parameters for staff planning so that, in the end, the district's priorities come from the staff and the community.

On the next few pages, we'll outline the ABCs of educational planning and marketing, and help you understand the steps you'll need to take, the preparation involved, and the activities in which you'll be engaged. Then we'll take you through the process, step-by step.

A. Planning at the policy level

Planning begins with the superintendent and the school board. It's their role to assess the status quo and to develop the vision that will guide the organization on its journey toward the future.

You'll begin this step in The MDS process by expanding your perspectives on the environment in which your school district functions. Leaders need to understand the context that is created by continuous change and the implication such change has for the school district.

You can develop a broad-based perspective by analyzing:

- ▮ The state, national, and international environment. You should assess major demographic shifts, economic conditions, the political climate, and technological advances and discoveries which can impact your organization.

■ Change forces. Engage people in a dialogue on the implications they have for your school district.

■ The local environment. This assessment will help you identify the unique elements of the local environment, internally and externally. It will also help you understand the readiness of people to change.

At the school board-superintendent level, The MDS process will help you:

■ determine what a great school district looks like;
■ draft a vision statement for your organization;
■ define the school district's mission;
■ assess school board effectiveness; and,
■ reaffirm the role of and establish goals for the school board.

The direct contact time with the school board and superintendent in this step of The MDS is approximately 3-4 hours.

B. Planning at the building and responsibility area level.

Once the direction of the school district has been established by it's vision and mission, you'll assemble teams from each building and responsibilty area.

These teams will be brought together to:

■ learn about the forces of change and the changing educational environment;

■ identify districtwide goals for consideration by the superintendent and school board; and,

■ draft priorities or goals for their building or responsibility area.

These planning and implementation teams should be broad-based, representing all segments of the staff and community. Most buildings need a planning team of 5-7 members.

The planning teams will present the priorities they develop to their colleagues in their respective buildings or responsibility areas. Once the priorities are approved at the site level, the teams will facilitate an implementation plan -- determining who will do what by when to address the priorities.

The superintendent and school board will review the districtwide priorities drafted by the teams and use them to write and adopt 4-6 goals for the school district.

The direct contact time with teams in this step is approximately one day.

C. Marketing the school district

You'll begin the marketing process the same way you started the planning process -- with analysis.

Team members will learn the concepts of marketing, targeting, and positioning. Then they'll use The MDS process to ...

- identify marketable assets at the district, building, and responsibility area levels. During this step you'll determine what your school district provides that people need and want. This assessment also will help you determine those things people need and want that your school district *doesn't* provide ... and those things your district provides that people *don't* want.

- identify marketing priorities at the district and building levels.

The marketing priorities will be processed by team members in their respective buildings and responsibility areas. And the superintendent will review the suggested districtwide marketing priorities and present them to the school board for adoption.

The direct contact time with teams in this step of The MDS process is one-half day.

On the following pages, we'll take you through The MDS process step-by step.

The ABCs of planning and marketing
Step-by-step

The ABCs of planning and marketing
Step-by-step

The prelude to planning

Planning can't take place in a vacuum. Nor can proactive change. That's why it's important to engage members of the staff and community in a dialogue about the future.

School staff members and people in the community often have different perspectives about change. Some resist it, hoping that "this too shall pass." Others relate change to logistics, such as getting chalk into the classroom in a timely manner. And, at the far end of the continuum, are those for whom change stimulates visions of intergalactic learning. Most people fall somewhere between these extremes. That's why it is important to create a frame of reference for planning with an "introduction to change." The goal in the introduction is to broaden the perspectives and stimulate the thinking of as many people as possible -- to paint a big picture about the nature of change, its dimensions, and its implications.

Objectives of the introduction

The purpose of the introduction is to broaden perspectives for future-oriented thinking and planning. In the first meeting with the school board and superintendent, and in the first meeting with staff teams, help people develop a better understanding of the problems and opportunities that face your schools.

Participants should hear about the challenges facing your schools, that the environment dictates changes , and that fulfilling the mission of the educational enterprise is too important and complex to be accommodated by quick-fix solutions.

During this phase of The MDS process, your objectives should include:

- exposing staff and community to change forces -- particularly those which have implications for your schools;

- creating consensus on the need for change;

- sharing concerns about the nature of change and the problems and opportunities it presents; and,

- building a foundation of support for the change process.

Procedure

Think of the introduction to change as the kick-off for your planning. The idea is to broaden understanding and perspective.

Who?   Ideally, you should expose all members of your staff and community to your introduction. The next best alternative is *all* staff and community leaders. Third best is staff representatives and community leaders.

Whatever your audience, you must communicate the change message through a variety of media. In fact, those who participate will be an important medium for disseminating information for you.

When?   Position the kick-off as a significant event. That's why the room you select and its set-up are important considerations.

Where?   Find a place where people can sit at round tables. You want to create an environment that stimulates conversation and camaraderie. Treat your participants as guests!

Tools?
- Put notepads at each place.
- Be sure to use quality projection equipment and a large screen.

■ Make sure that the microphone works before you begin.

■ Have coffee, tea, juice, and fruit in the room.

To prepare: Use the *Change Forces* material as the focal point of your presentation.

You can use this material to supplement your introduction to change. In addition, use headlines from any of the regularly published education newspapers or journals. In any given week, the news headlines can demonstrate the diversity of influences on today's schools.

Topics: Begin your presentation with a big-perspective overview. Your objectives are to talk about changes that are occurring in the marketplace and to invite people to think about the implications for your schools. This is the place to help people understand the myriad influences on the educational enterprise.

End this segment by pointing out that most of the forces that trigger change are external to the organization, whether it's public or private. Point to the news headlines as an example. Odds are overwhelming that none of the headlines in the educational newspapers of record will refer to your school district, yet many of them have potential for impacting your schools or influencing the way you operate. A court decision, a crisis elsewhere, a discovery, new legislation -- all are external factors that educators must accommodate in their planning and management routines.

In the second segment of your presentation, shift your focus to the customers of education. Most people don't know that education's clients have changed. For instance, learners have become younger and older at the same time. They are more ethnically diverse than they used to be, and they have heterogeneous beliefs, attitudes, and opinions.

When people think of our educational customers, too many still think of Ozzie and Harriet or the Cleavers sending their youngsters off to school and welcoming them home at the end of the day. But these families (working father, stay-at-home mom, and two or more children) represent less than 7% of U.S. households. Nearly 3/4 of the mothers of school-age children are now in the for-pay workforce.

The dual-career family is a significant change in education's consumer base. Like it or not, it has made "baby-sitting" an important role for schools. It has helped spur tremendous growth in child care centers, preschool programs, and latchkey services. And it has forced schools to offer parent conferences during both the day and the evening, has changed volunteerism, and, for the most part, has eliminated the idea of having "homeroom mothers."

Add to this the increasing heterogeneity of the population, the agendas of various interest groups, the demands of business, the need for lifelong learning, and the mental set of a generation that has been raised under the influence of television, and it's apparent that education not only has more customers, but it also has more diverse customers.

Thus far, the kick-off has focused on broad brush pictures of change and challenge. While it's important that people have this overall perspective, "What about us? is a legitimate bottom line question. To make your introduction relevant to your audience, end your presentation with a specific look at forces in *your* marketplace.

- Develop a demographic profile of your students and the community served by your school. Highlight the changes.

- Compile a list of staff concerns and talk about it.

■ Show how attitudes about teachers, homework, and learning have changed.

■ Let people know how the information explosion has had an impact on your school, and how technology either has been or must be integrated into your curriculum.

■ In other words, give people a look at your school within the context of the bigger picture.

End your introductory meeting by telling participants that you are beginning a planning process designed to help your school district capitalize on change.

Let them know that you need their support and input on this journey toward a better tomorrow.

A: Planning at the policy level

Remember that vision and mission come from the top. They are typically set by the school board and superintendent, but they are not set in a vacuum. They are set in the context of the change forces and factors that are internal and external to the school district.

As with most other tasks in *The ABC Complete Book of School Marketing*, this one can be handled by a member of the staff or an external facilitator ... or a combination of the two. Do whatever will work for you.

But, remember to be honest with yourself. If you assign responsibility for this process to someone on the staff you may be asking for the impossible. There aren't many staff members who have the facilitation skills to successfully implement a process like this -- especially on their own turf.

For the best results, we recommend an internal "point person" and an external facilitator/consultant. If you do opt to proceed with an internal facilitator, make sure that person understands *The Market-Driven System*® and has proven facilitating skills. (For more information, see *Guidelines for facilitating* in Appendix B).

Whatever you do, don't trust any exercise in The MDS process to the luck of the draw by calling for volunteers to lead it.

Objectives

During this phase of the process, your objectives are to ...

- ▌ identify the dimensions of a truly great school district;

- ▌ subjectively rate your school district's status on each of the dimensions;

- ▌ draft vision and mission statements;

- ▌ conduct a school board self-evaluation; and,

- ▌ set goals for members of the school board.

Procedure

When?   Plan on a three-hour meeting with the school board and superintendent. It can begin with a deli sandwich at six o'clock; adjournment guaranteed by 9:15 p.m. If every one can't make the meeting, reschedule it. Your school board can't function as a team if half the team is missing.

Tools?   Duplicate copies of the *Dimensions of greatness* form in *Appendix A*. Have an overhead projector, blank transparencies, and a flip chart.

What?   Start the meeting with a refresher or update on change forces and their implications. There are a couple of reasons for beginning with such a presentation. First, it provides information people need. Second, it helps participants get oriented to the planning process.

Activity 1   Using the *Dimensions of greatness* form from *Appendix A*, ask each member of the school board to write down what he or she believes are the dimensions of a truly great school district. For example, if a board member believes a truly great school district is characterized by "a well trained staff," that characteristic should be written on the form, as in the example in Exhibit A.

Board members should rate each dimension they identify in terms of *where our school district is now* by using a zero-to-ten scale. (Zero is low; ten is high.) Continuing the example, an individual participant might list "a well trained staff" as a dimension of a truly great school district and give it a rating of 6 (or 2 or 8) on the 10-point scale.

EXHIBIT A

The Dimensions of Greatness

well-trained staff   Low 0 - 1 - 2 -3 - 4 - 5 - 6 - 7 - 8 - 9 -10 High

supportive community   Low 0 - 1 - 2 -3 - 4 - 5 - 6 - 7 - 8 - 9 -10 High

motivated students   Low 0 - 1 - 2 -3 - 4 - 5 - 6 - 7 - 8 - 9 -10 High

_____   Low 0 - 1 - 2 -3 - 4 - 5 - 6 - 7 - 8 - 9 -10 High

_____   Low 0 - 1 - 2 -3 - 4 - 5 - 6 - 7 - 8 - 9 -10 High

After no more than five minutes of working alone, each board member should be asked to share his/her list of dimensions and ratings. The meeting facilitator should simply record them on a overhead for all to see.

When each board member has reported, the facilitator should ask if anyone would like to add any other dimension to the list.

This is a wonderful communication exercise. It helps board members understand one another, and it allows the superintendent to see what kinds of things are on the agenda of individual board members.

Identifying dimensions of greatness is also a good way to learn what people value in your school district. (When people identify what they believe are the dimensions of a truly great school, they provide a clear indication of what they value in a school.)

There usually isn't any need to comment on the dimensions. Simply list them, make sure participants understand them, and move to Activity 2.

Put your facilitator hat on. This exercise also can be used to gather information from and to gain understanding of the staff and community. It can be used to enhance the staff and community forums described in *Prelude to planning*. Principals can use it with their staff members to identify the dimensions of a truly great *school*. The *Dimensions of greatness* form has a variety of applications as a stand-alone activity. It provides people with a comfortable vehicle for expressing their opinions, and it provides marketplace intelligence for your planning process.

Activity 2   In this activity, the Board moves from assessing to establishing direction as they draft a vision statement for the school district.

Tools?   Use the *Organizational vision* form in *Appendix A* for this activity.

What?   A vision statement tells where the school district is headed. It is a future-oriented, written picture of the best that can be.

Good vision statements are inspirational. They provide a directional perspective that is essential for effective thinking, planning, and marketing. They communicate where school district resources will be focused.

Here's a sample vision statement you can share:

> *It is our vision to create an exemplary school district that is acknowledged for the caliber of its graduates, the quality of its staff, and the diversity of its programs.*

Note that the sample vision statement is short -- in this case, one sentence. The idea is to produce something that people can remember and articulate.

In *Appendix B* you'll find other vision statements you can share. Invite board members to copy them, edit them, or use them as idea generators. (We tell board members there are more than 15,000 school districts in America. Then we ask them if they really believe they are going to develop a vision statement that contains elements no one has thought of before. While they still don't like copying, this thought makes them a little less adverse to editing, and a whole lot more willing to avoid "re-inventing the wheel.")

Ask board members to envision your school district functioning at optimum. Have them describe what they see in their minds. Write down the key words on the overhead. Then tell the board members that you will draft a vision statement that captures the essence of their thinking. Tell them you'll send this to them in a few days. In turn, they'll have a few days to react to it, suggesting additions or deletions ... or approving it as is.

We like to tell board members not to be offended if their exact wording is missing from the vision statement. We also tell them it's unlikely that all their thoughts will be described in the vision statement (because no one wants a six-page vision statement that will be shelved somewhere in a three-ring binder!). Tell board members you will take license in capturing the essence of their thinking; ask them to understand why this must be.

Activity 3   This activity focuses on developing a mission statement.

Tools?   Use the *Organizational mission* form in *Appendix B.*

What?   The goal is to produce a short statement of organizational purpose. Mission statements are present in their orientation, and provide a response to the question, *"What do you do?"*

Here's a sample mission statement:

> *It is our mission to provide quality educational services to learners of all ages, aspirations, and abilities.*

Note the difference between vision and mission statements. Vision statements are future-oriented. They describe the ideas, and tell where the district is headed. Mission statements focus on the present; they tell what you do now.

Optional
Activity   An optional -- although most worthwhile -- activity at this point is a school board self-evaluation. As the board prepares to address the changing marketplace, it's appropriate that board members reflect on their strengths and weaknesses.

While there are questionnaires and other techniques for this purpose, here's an easy and effective way to conduct a board self-evaluation. Give each member of the school board a copy of the *Dimensions of greatness* form. Ask each member to write the dimensions of a truly great school board. For example, one board member might believe a truly great school board "comes to meetings well prepared." That member would write these words on the form and then rate how the board is doing now on that dimension. Use the zero-to-ten scale as before. Allow board members 4-5 minutes to work alone. Then have them share what they have written.

Once every board member has reported and the facilitator has recorded everyone's thoughts on an overhead or flip chart, show members the *Characteristics of effective school boards* summary which appears in *Appendix B*. Ask them what they think about the dimensions and ratings they produced and the characteristics on the list.

Activity 4   Setting goals for the school board is the final exercise in Part A of The MDS. Say this to members of the board: "Given the changes we described, the dimensions of greatness you identified, the vision and mission you have in mind, and the self-evaluation we just completed, what would be three or four appropriate goals for the school board? Remember the goals we want will be for the members of the school board, no one else." Use the *Goals for organizational leaders* form in *Appendix A*.

Here are two sample school board goals:

> *To establish a forum in which there can be more discussions of substance on educational matters.*
>
> *To improve the school board's decision-making process.*

As you did with the vision and mission statements, tell board members you will take what they have said and craft four or five goal statements for them to review. Send the drafts to board members, giving them a week or so to suggest changes, additions, and/or deletions ... or to accept them as is.

This final activity is important because it allows board members to establish priorities which are related to their policy-setting role. Setting goals at the board level also sends a positive message to members of the staff and community.

B: Responsibility area planning

Once organizational direction has been defined, it's time to work the process through the system -- to seek input while building ownership and commitment.

Objectives

During this phase, your objectives are to:

■ introduce more people to the nature of change and its implications;

■ seek multiple perspectives on the dimensions of greatness;

■ share the school district's vision and mission, and the school board goals; and

■ identify districtwide and building level/departmental priorities.

Procedure

Who?   Because it's usually impossible (and inefficient) to gather all employees and key stakeholders, we advocate assembling teams from the district's school buildings and/or departments. A typical team should have 5-7 members.

Have principals (or department directors) select the team members.

Make sure that the teams include the principal, a teacher, and a support staff member. The balance of the team membership should be whatever best serves the building. There might be two teachers, a secretary, and a custodian ... or a parent and citizen without school-age children ... or a community leader or student or business person.

The key is to have appropriate representation. In addition, it's important that each member of the team be a high credibility, "high speed" person. The members of the team will be explaining *The Market-Driven System®* to their colleagues and sharing what they propose for the school or department. It makes sense that these people should be the best available.

When?   Plan on having a solid block of time; e.g., from 8 a.m. until 2 p.m.

Tools?   An overhead projector, blank acetate sheets, marking pens, and copies of the *Dimensions of greatness, What's wrong, right, and wonderful?*, and *Organizational priorities, objectives, and activities* forms from *Appendix A*. Each team should have its own table. Have refreshments available; provide lunch.

What?   Begin by underlining the importance of the meeting and expressing gratitude to those who are participating.

Next, present the introductory comments you used in the *Prelude to planning*. Give participants an overview of the change forces and their implications. Localize the implications whenever possible. Present survey data if you have it. The idea is to provide a comprehensive briefing which establishes a broad perspective for planning.

Activity 1   Have participants identify what they believe are the dimensions of a truly great school district. Give each team five or six minutes to develop a list. Have someone from the team report as the facilitator records the responses and ratings on an overhead. When all the teams have reported, show them the dimensions of greatness developed by the school board. People are usually surprised at the similarity of dimensions and ratings, and they begin to better understand that everyone wants the same thing for the clients of the school district.

Activity 2   Give each team copies of the *What's wrong, right, and wonderful?* form. Ask them to think about the school district, and to spend five or six minutes responding to each of the questions on the form. Follow with group reports.

Activity 3   Now give each team copies of the *Organizational priorities* form in *Appendix A*. Give each team member a white copy to use for notes. Give each team leader one blue copy and three yellow copies.

Ask the team to identify, using the blue form, one districtwide priority. Here's an example:

> *To develop a comprehensive staff development program.*

Then, using the yellow forms, ask team members to identify up to three priorities for their building or department.

Tell team members not to spend time working on the final wording of their priorities. Ask them to focus on communicating the essence of their thinking. Tell them you'll collect their notes at the end of the activity and draft their priorities for them.

Here are a couple of examples of building-level priority statements or goals:

> *To use technology to enhance human capacity and learning at the classroom level.*
>
> *To position the high school as a lifelong learning center.*
>
> *To articulate the math curriculum across grade levels.*

To conclude the day, have team leaders share the district and building-level priorities identified by their teams.

Now it's the facilitator's job to collect all the *Organizational priorities* worksheets and develop drafts of the priorities identified by the teams.

When this is done, the facilitator should send the draft priorities and original worksheets back to members of the building teams. Team members, in turn, should review the draft and make any changes which they believe are appropriate.

Then team members should explain to their building-level colleagues what transpired at the planning meeting. Next they should share the priorities they developed and ask their staff colleagues for "buy in." At this point the dialogue can result in complete buy in, changes in wording, or the addition or deletion of one or more priorities. Once the staff reaches consensus on the priorities, have the team leaders send a final copy to the facilitator.

When all the buildings have submitted their priorities, the facilitator and superintendent can review and compare them with the districtwide change priorities suggested by teams. From this material the facilitator and superintendent identify four-to-six appropriate priorities for the district. These priorities are presented by the superintendent to the school board for consideration and adoption.

The building teams now can orchestrate the development and implementation of specific plans at the building level. They should start by completing the *Organzational objectives* and *Organizational activities* forms.

Think about what has happened during Parts A and B of *The Market-Driven System®*. We began at the policy level by determining the district's direction. Then we asked the representatives from each building and department to help us move in that direction by identifying priorities. Finally, we used the material from the staff to create districtwide priorities. In summary, we implemented a strategic planning process that is top-down, bottom-up. We allowed everyone to play an appropriate role. And we built ownership and commitment in the organization's future.

C: Marketing the organization

You can't market a bad school. You have to fix it first. And if you have a good school, it's wise to make it better. Then you can market even more effectively. Remember, our purpose in marketing is to create and keep customers.

Objectives

During this phase, your objectives are to:

- identify the marketable assets of the school district;

- identify key target audiences in the school district;

- move toward establishing an identity for the school district; and,

- design marketing activities at the building and department levels.

Procedure

What?   Building and departmental teams should be assembled for a half-day. Give them an introduction to the concepts of marketing, targeting, and positioning, and begin drafting marketing initiatives at the building level.

Tools?   Use the marketing related forms in *Appendix A*. You'll need white copies of all the forms for everyone, and one blue copy and three yellow copies of *Marketing priorities* form for each team.

Activity 1   The first activity calls for team members to identify the marketable assets of the school district. These assets should be placed in two categories: things people need and things people want. Identify one or more target audiences for each asset.

Next, the teams should identify who else in the community or service area has the same assets as the school district, and discuss why people should "buy" from you instead of them. This exercise results in a picture of what the district has to market, a list of prospective "buyers," and an assessment of competitive advantage. (Note that *analysis* is also the first step in the marketing process!)

Activity 2   With the assessment of marketable assets completed, have each team use the *The marketing planner* form to brainstorm what the district could market. Then use the form to make a list of the people to whom you would market, explain why you would market to them, and identify the position you'd like to establish.

Activity 3   To conclude Part C, use the *Marketing priorities* form to identify one thing that should be marketed at the district level and up to three things that should be marketed at the building level.

End the session with a report from each team. Again, the facilitator should collect the forms, edit the material, and send drafts back to the teams, processing the *Marketing priorities* form in the same manner as the *Organizational prioritie*s form.

A few words about evaluation

Evaluation brings certainty to the process. It enables you to identify which priorities were attained and which were not. It also helps you continue the pursuit of strategies that are working while you fix those that aren't.

Facilitators and team leaders should use the *Evaluation* form in *Appendix A* to:

▌ identify the pluses and minuses associated with each activity;

▌ analyze the factors which led to attainment or non-attainment of each activity; and

■ strengthen the plan as it transitions from evaluation to a re-analysis of the strategic environment.

Evaluative data comes from tallying the pluses and minuses of each activity in the planning and marketing process. Then the pluses and minuses are analyzed so that the factors which led to attainment or non-attainment of the priorities can be clearly identified.

The nature of the evaluation system is ongoing. As pluses and minuses are noted, team members and their staff colleagues can make necessary corrections in the plan. In addition, we suggest that team members be called together every six months to share what has and hasn't worked -- and to celebrate their successes.

The concepts of marketing, targeting, and positioning

The concepts of
marketing, targeting, and positioning

Theodore Levitt says the purpose of marketing is to create and keep a customer. To address that purpose requires a conceptual framework for marketing, targeting, and positioning.

We like to think of marketing as an umbrella concept that covers everything from conception of an idea, program, or product to its delivery and use. And, as the umbrella is opened over ideas, programs, and products, marketers need to employ a strategy.

Should you take a proactive leadership position and aggressively market yourself as *the* best place to learn? Or should you relinquish the leadership role to someone else and base what you do on what they do? Or should you continually try end runs? Or should you play sniper, watching for opportunities and seizing them as they occur.

The problem is that you can't employ just any strategy that strikes your fancy. Market leaders, for example, tend to be most successful using aggressive, proactive strategies. Leader wannabes usually base what they do on what the leader does. Their strategies -- and there is nothing wrong with this -- are more reactive in nature.

End run strategies are usually employed to bring something new to the market. The strategy allows those who aren't market leaders to assume a piece of leadership action. For example, while General Motors remains the dominant auto manufacturer, Chrysler did an end run with mini vans, eventually acquiring a leadership position in that market niche.

Sniper strategies typically are employed by those who are not market leaders. They are used to capitalize on the moment. For example, there are companies that can turnout a paperback book overnight. They use this capacity to get what they can from the marketplace before addressing the next market opportunity. They usually are not a long-term threat to mainstream publishing houses.

Playwright Woody Allen said timing is everything. That's certainly true in the world of marketing, and it implies that, while you may have an overall strategy, there are situations which may dictate using a substrategy. There may be a little sniper in everyone!

The Marketing Strategies	Used by
1. Lead dog	∎ Marketplace leaders
2. I spy	∎ Leader wannabes
3. End run	∎ Those who are pursuing a market niche
4. Sniper	∎ People who are capitalizing on the moment

Be careful not to fool yourself

Everyone wants to be *the* market leader. But that's not possible -- everyone can't be *the* leader.

Try this: Write down the names of the five best school districts in your state. Use whatever criteria you want. Ask a few friends to do the same. Consolidate the lists into a master.

Now look over the master list. Is your district on it? (What are the common denominators of those who are on the list? We'll bet none is in an impoverished community!)

Your list may be more perception than reality. Some of the districts, in fact, may not be among the best in the state. But, then, in the world of marketing, the perception *is* the reality.

People act on what they think and believe, and what they think and believe may be a long way from reality. The school districts on your list should be using a lead dog marketing strategy.

If your school district isn't on the list, you should be using one of the other three marketing strategies (or some combination thereof). Don't fool yourself by confusing the goal (attainment of objectives that lead to people perceiving you as a market leader) with the reality (that you presently aren't perceived as a market leader).

How do you target?

The second of the key concepts is targeting. This conceptual frame implies that some people care more about your message (program, idea, product, service) than others. That leads to a simple (and sometimes painful) question: *Who cares?*

The way to start marketing is to look into the marketplace and ask, *Who really cares about this message (program, idea, product, service)?* The answer to the question is the target.

In a way, targeting says some people are more important than others. From a marketing perspective, that's true. You'll probably never see Mercedes Benz commercials during the Saturday morning cartoons. The reason: their market research (analysis!) probably indicates that viewers of cartoons don't purchase too many luxury automobiles. In this case, people watching cartoons are less important than others in the marketplace.

Targeting dictates that you look at what you have to offer to the marketplace, and ask, *Who cares?* For example,

What do you have to offer?	**Who cares about this?**
1. latchkey programs	∎ working parents
2. preschool programs	∎ working parents ∎ parents who believe in early childhood education ∎ parents who believe it's important to give their child a jump on kindergarten
3. third grade reading	∎ parents of third graders ∎ parents of youngsters in grades K, 1, 2

You also can use the targeting question (*Who cares?*) to do a quick assessment of your publications and the mix of vehicles you use to deliver your messages.

A districtwide newsletter which is sent to everyone in the school district can be targeted. For example, the article on the left front of the cover page is the one people look at first. This is the most important physical location on page one of the newsletter. Hence, the most important general interest article should appear here (and that's typically *not* the superintendent's column ... or the principal's!).

Next, put something of interest to elementary parents above the masthead. Then, try to appeal to those without school-age children in the right hand column.

Put a box at the bottom of the left hand column. Use the box to tell readers what's inside the publication. They'll look for something they care about and turn to it. This means you need to spend time thinking about (*analyzing!*) your audiences and what appeals to them. This important planning step will enable you to target every article in your publication to someone.

If targeting messages ups the odds of people reading what you want them to read, a related consideration also deserves attention, and that's the mix of vehicles or media you use to deliver messages. Marketing people call this the marketing mix.

Generally, if you are trying to build awareness of a subject, the vehicles of choice are newspapers, radio, and television -- the mass media. While you're interested in letting everyone know about the subject, the reality is that not everyone cares. That, in fact, is why newspapers have sections such as business, sports, lifestyle, etc. And that is why want ads are categorized or targeted. Can you imagine sifting through all the want ads to find out who is trying to sell a Golden Retriever?

Nonetheless, you can use the mass media to build awareness in target audiences! For example, you can build awareness of a new middle school program by placing an article or story with the mass media. Your targets may be elementary and middle school parents. Consider anyone else who reads the article a bonus.

The mass media build awareness. Typically stories or articles which appear in the newspaper or on radio or television provide an overview of a subject. They don't contain too much detail. (Ask yourself how much detail about the latest controversy a reporter on the steps of the nation's capitol can provide during a 20-second television story.)

As your informational effort shifts from one of building awareness to one of gaining support and commitment, your messages need to become more personal. This means that your messages need to be targeted to address the informational needs and wants of specific groups of people (targets). This, in turn, means that your messages will become more specific and will be delivered through such media as brochures, on-line computer services, personal letters, or by telephone. The degree to which you target your message and the variety of media you employ depends on your communication objectives.

Obviously, your message can have many targets and the message can be delivered to the targets through a variety of media. But what message are you trying to deliver, and to whom are you trying to deliver it? The *Media mix* form in *Appendix B* will help you plan your targeting strategy. That leads to the third concept -- positioning.

What's a position?

It's advertisingese for your image or identity. It's what people think about when they think about you.

When people think about Chevy trucks, they think about vehicles that are built "like a rock." They know Folgers coffee is "Mountain grown." And they love Campbell's soup because it's "Mmmm mmmm good." Each of these statements is used to position the product in a target's mind -- to create an image or identity.

When positions are firmly established in the public mind, the product and the positioning statement often become interchangeable. The night time cold medicine is Nyquil, and Nyquil is the night time cold medicine. When people think about a cold medicine to take at night, many think about Nyquil, and when they think about Nyquil, they think about the night time cold medicine.

People still say "Will you Xerox this?" when they want a copy, or "May I have a Kleenex?" instead of asking for a tissue.

To establish a position or identity, you need to assess the competitive advantage you have in the marketplace. Why, for example, should people come to your preschool program instead of the one down the street? Here it helps to look at several things simultaneously -- what you have to offer, the pluses and minuses of what you have to offer, the target(s), and the key messages which will appeal to each target.

If your preschool program is high quality, that's a plus. If the program is located in a shabby facility, that's a minus. If the program is expensive, that could be a plus or a minus ... or even a neutral. Let's develop a scenario. First, everyone wants quality. We could be proactive/aggressive in marketing that value. But what about the facility? A shabby building doesn't appeal to many people, but maybe it's appearance can be over come by the quality of the program ... or the proximity to those who will attend. But what about cost? Again, it depends. Some people believe that you get what you pay for. They believe high quality and high price go hand in hand. For them the message is quality and price, and, maybe, closeness. Others may not care about cost for a different reason. They just want a quality educational experience for their child (and the fact that it's nearby can be another plus). It depends. This is why marketing people engage in consumer research -- to find out what depends.

The final strategic step, then, is to position the preschool program. Start by making a list of potential target audiences. Then identify their needs and wants. And then ask ...

- ∎ What key messages will appeal to each target audience?

- ∎ What identity do I have with each target audience now?

- ∎ Would I change these identities if I could?

- ∎ How would I change these identities?

- ∎ Given all this, how should I position my preschool program with each target audience?

As you do this exercise, make sure you ask what each target audience has to offer you. You may find, for example, that one target group is so small it's not worth *your* time and energy to communicate with the people who compose it.

The forms in *Appendix A* will help you work through these questions as you design an effective marketing program for your program (school, idea, product, service).

Be believable ... and first

Identities exist in the public mind. Hallmark talks about the cards you mail "when you care enough to send the very best." They engage in lead dog marketing strategies to reinforce their position as a marketplace leader. They produce high quality products. And, so, the product and the position converge in the public mind to create a positive image of "the very best."

If Hallmark produced low quality greeting cards on paper stock that contained chunks of wood, their positioning statement wouldn't work. It simply wouldn't be believable.

The same is true for schools. You can't claim to be the very best if you are something less. Just as you can't market a bad product, you can't market a bad school.

Before you adopt a positioning statement or slogan for your schools, ask yourself if the statement is true. Then ask if it's believable. Finally, ask if anyone else is using the same statement. In positioning, the ideal message is true, believable, and first. You can't position your school district as the one with the highest test scores if, in fact, it does not have the highest scores. You can't position your school as the best in the universe because -- no matter how good you are -- people won't believe you are the best in the universe. And it doesn't do any good to say you "bring good things to life" or that you're "creating a higher standard." Those positions have already been established in the public mind, and people know they refer to General Electric and Cadillac, respectively.

Marketing in action
A case study

Marketing in action
A case study

XYZ School District -- Marketing assessment

About the district

With a K-12 enrollment of approximately 6,000 students, XYZ School District is the largest school district in the area. The district has elementary schools, ranging from 400-600 in student population. Each elementary school provides instruction to students in kindergarten through fifth grade. Two of the elementary schools operate a pre-kindergarten program for children with special needs.

All students in the district attend one of two middle schools. The middle schools serve students in grades 6, 7 and 8. Both middle schools use team teaching for the delivery of instruction.

One high school, XYZ High School, is operated by the district. This building serves students in grade nine through 12. XYZ High School staff are proud of the fact that their building was named an exemplary school five years ago.

XYZ High School employs a "schools within a school" organizational plan. Four pods are located around a central core. The core contains, a library, auditorium, cafeteria and band, chorus and music rooms. Students are assigned alphabetically by grade to the pods. Course offerings include a rigorous college preparatory curriculum, a highly successful advanced placement program, and a Tech Prep Program articulated with the local community college. The advanced placement program at XYZ High School offers advanced placement courses in English, history, calculus, chemistry, mathematics, and computer science.

All schools in the XYZ School District have active parent-teacher organizations, and parents are encouraged to visit the schools, volunteer in the classrooms, and become an integral part of their child's education.

All schools have computer labs and many classrooms have their own computers. Integration of technology is high on the district's agenda.

The district has been doing "okay" and wants to continue to be "okay" under the new "charter/choice" legislation due to take effect in six months. That legislation will enable parents to send their child to any school in the state. Before the effective date of the legislation, parents must notify the XYZ School District whether their child will remain in the school district or be attending another school of the parent's choice.

The district administrators want to build upon the district's current enrollment base by using the people and resources on hand to work toward clearly defined objectives. Areas of focus include communications, both internal and external, personnel, parental support, funding, and community relations.

About the community

The district serves a small urban area which is surrounded by suburbia and farms. Occupations of parents range from government to business to light manufacturing and farming. The population is approximately 50% minorities. The district appears to have a senior citizen population (ages 65+) that is growing.

The community is diverse, economically healthy, and relatively prosperous. It is a retail center for the area, and several major corporations are located within the district's boundaries.

About the organization of the district

The average experience of present board members of the XYZ School District is three years. It appears, based on staff comments, that management (administration) is "top-down."

Both teachers and custodians are represented by labor organizations. The teacher union is perceived as "a 1970s type of union," with a very strong "old guard" core -- particularly evident at the high school. All leadership positions in the union are filled by high school teachers.

<u>**Beginning the process of marketing**</u>

In light of the charter/choice legislation from the state, a self-assessment survey was taken of the elementary, middle, and high school staffs. Through the assessment, staff members were asked to reflect on their individual schools and identify:

- *What's wrong* and needs to be fixed?
- *What's right* and needs to be maintained?
- *What's wonderful* and should be made even better?

District support staff and administrative staff were also asked to respond to the same questions. Staff members were told that the information they provided would be used to pinpoint strengths and weaknesses at the building and district levels. It would also be used to formulate a marketing plan for the district.

What staff members had to say about their building or district

Comments of employees were diverse. Elementary and middle school staff members responded at great length and in detail to each question. The comments of the high school staff, however, were less detailed and tended to be more negative. As a group, high school staff members tended not to identify what they could do to improve the high school or the district.

Following is a composite of the responses. Within each category are the responses in descending order of frequency mentioned.

XYZ School District: What's wrong and needs to be fixed

1. *Communication*

   - lack of communication between administration and staff
   - left hand doesn't know what the right hand is doing
   - rumors abound
   - lack of communication between staff of administration center and buildings
   - poor public image

2. *Working relationships*

- lack of respect for staff, internally and externally
- lack of teacher input in decision-making processes
- lack of respect for professionalism of teachers
- lack of honesty and trust
- employee negativity
- tendency of staff to "show and tell" internal problems
- all staff members need to treat parents with respect
- more supervision is needed of new teachers
- need to hold all employees accountable for success of district

3. *Building conditions*

- regular/routine building maintenance
- daily cleaning of facilities
- obvious repair needs are not being addressed

4. *Instructional concerns*

- planning time is insufficient
- lack of time for teams to plan together
- need more supplies and materials for instruction
- improve and update instructional strategies
- student behavior
- need to establish a districtwide discipline policy that is structured and uniform
- avoid jumping on the bandwagon regarding instructional theories
- parents need to become more involved in their child's education
- parent training needs to be offered to help parents help children learn
- need more emphasis on linking courses together -- from elementary to high school
- need for more focused professional development opportunities for all staff

XYZ School District: What's right and needs to be maintained

1. Staff -- dedicated, caring, adaptive, and dedicated to meeting the needs of all students

2. Parental involvement at the elementary level

3. Technology -- availability of computers and software

4. Special programs for students, including

    ■ gifted and talented
    ■ student recognition programs
    ■ diversity of class offerings at the middle school level
    ■ varied programs at high school (advanced placement, arts, etc.)
    ■ special education programming
    ■ after-school programs and club activities

5. Curriculum improvement process

6. Professional development opportunities for staff

7. Administrative support -- administrative staff is supportive, accessible and concerned

XYZ School District: What's wonderful and should be made even better

1. Educators, teachers, staff -- educators are willing to go beyond the call of duty to put children first

2. Innovative programs

    ■ diversity of programs
    ■ exploratory focus
    ■ special education
    ■ gifted and talented
    ■ foreign languages
    ■ multi-age classrooms
    ■ after-school activities and extracurricular activities
    ■ latchkey programs and child care

- advanced placement classes
- vocational programs

3. Computers and new technology

4. Progressive district

5. Caring administrative staff

6. Staff development opportunities

7. Developing an integrated curriculum

8. Diversity of curriculum

9. Parent involvement

What would you do?

Of course, there are no right answers or guaranteed solutions to the case study. But, given the staff assessment and the fact that legislation which would permit parents to send their child to any school in the area would take effect in six months, the district developed the following frame for its activities:

1. Write off the high school. There wasn't time to spend convincing the high school staff that they should become actively engaged in marketing activities. For the first year, it was decided to "let the markletplace prevail," in effect testing the we're good and we don't need to market-theory of the high school teachers.

2. Target marketing initiatives at the preschool and elementary level. Teachers and other staff members at these levels were anxious about the impending legislation, and eager to enhance the image of their schools.

3. Adopt the *Champions for Children*® program. This ready-to-go program could be used to reinforce the position desired by the preschool and elementary staff.

4. Personal marketing activities would be initiated at the preschool and elementary levels. (See Section 14.)

5. Every teacher would develop a teacher book. (See Appendix C.)

6. Teachers would receive training in effective parent conference. The goal was to make this semiannual event one which was characterized by the best conferences ever.

7. Survey the staff, parents, and other members of the community. (While this analytical step would have come first in an ideal world, the thinking was to get going with a marketing program and use the survey results to fine tune it. The other option would have been to wait for the survey results before initiating any marketing activities -- an option not considered given the timeline for activation of the legislation.)

8. Conduct a "See for Yourself" campaign, designed to get people into the schools so that they could see for themselves all the quality programs and services available to students.

9. Finally, there was agreement between the teachers union and the school board members that the school board meeting should cease to be a place where teachers and school board members crossed sabres, aired dirty laundry, and exchanged unpleasantries much to the delight of the reporters covering the meetings and at great expense to the district's image.

During the balance of the school year, more activities were added as a result of analyzing the survey results. But the initial activities did pay off. Most parents opted to leave their children enrolled in the school district. Ironically, the only loss of students because of choice was at the high school level.

Marketing in action
Champions for Children®

Marketing in action
Champions for Children®

The purpose of the program

The *Champions for Children*® program is the property of the National School Public Relations Association (NSPRA, 15948 Derwood Road, Rockville, MD 20855. Telephone 301.519.0496).

The program exists to improve conditions for children in America. That's being done with products and processes that help bring people together in the best interest of our nation's youngsters. Foremost on the agenda is anything that will improve educational opportunity.

The program is described here to provide readers with an example of a rather comprehensive marketing initiative.

The beginning

William J. Banach created the *Champions for Children*® program to help the New Hampshire Association of School Administrators (NHSAA) lead initiatives for young people in that state. Banach trained members of the Association in strategic thinking, planning, and marketing, giving them a framework for developing child-centered coalitions. In the training, he emphasized involving people in the educational process.

Did the program work?

NHSAA's Executive Director will tell you, "It was the most positive thing our Association has done in a decade." Now the program is being used by school districts and educational organizations across the country.

Rationale for the program

New Hampshire school administrators were disheartened by polls that showed low levels of support for public education and school leaders. They were concerned that distorted perceptions of schools limited their capacity to improve educational opportunities in the state.

To address these concerns, Banach worked with NHSAA to position administrators as *Champions for Children*®. He believed then – and does now – that communication about education should focus more on children and less about school finance and "educational excellence." In short, Banach made children the issue and challenged everyone to join in a crusade to benefit them.

Initial program components

The program began in a meeting of New Hampshire school administrators which was facilitated by Banach. Together, they identified what they meant when they said that they were *Champions for Children*®.

They defined the critical issues that faced New Hampshire education, and then they focused on themselves. They learned how to do a better job of listening to people, how to create visions and goals and community support for their schools, and how they could help others become *Champions for Children*®.

NHSAA also created "swat teams" to develop background briefings on critical issues facing New Hampshire children. The basic idea was to help educators seize the opportunity and respond to critics from a position of strength – as *Champions for Children*®.

As the program matured, child advocates united to support young people. At the same time, NHSAA advanced a child-centered agenda and facilitated a statewide sharing of ideas that benefited young people.

NHSAA also celebrated success ... by identifying and publicly saluting people who were doing good things for kids. Those who were honored came from all walks of life – from every corner of the state. They had just one thing in common – they were *Champions for Children*®.

The campaign evolves

As NHSAA members began implementing their plan, Banach expanded the *Champions for Children*® campaign. Largely as a result of information disseminated by the National School Public Relations Association, corporate affiliates, and various educational associations, the *Champions for Children*® program began to spread across North America.

Now there are various products to enhance the initiative and to support anyone who wants to champion children. As more school districts, agencies, and businesses affiliate with the campaign, new activities are proliferating:

- **In San Diego,** the San Diego County Office of Education has a television show titled *Champions for Children*®. The program features people from all walks of life who are doing things to benefit children. The same thing is happening in Yuma, Arizona.

- **In Illinois and Texas,** The Illinois Association of School Boards and the Texas Association of School Administrators have used *Champions for Children*® as the theme of their state conferences, and are championing children in school districts across the state.

- **In Wisconsin,** the Wisconsin School Board Association encouraged its membership to become *Champions for Children*® by conducting a sellout training program and awarding *Champions for Children*® lapel pins to more than 400 state convention attendees. The Wisconsin Association of School District Administrators featured *Champions for Children*® at its statewide *Summit for Children.*

- **In Ohio,** a local school district operates the Champion Child® preschool program.

- **In Minnesota,** state education associations have united under the *Champions for Children*® banner to strengthen their advocacy for public education.

- **In Pennsylvania,** a rock band held a benefit concert to raise money for a *Champions for Children*® educational foundation centered at the Capital Area Intermediate Unit. The Intermediate Unit also sponsored a *Champions for Children*® golf outing (and sold more than $3,000 worth of tee shirts to benefit their foundation).

- **And, nationally,** the American Association of School Administrators spotlighted *Champions for Children*® by giving the program "Distinguished Lecture" status at its annual conference.

Good ideas breed more good ideas

NSPRA is now encouraging *Champions for Children*® affiliates to network with one another. Campaign affiliates borrow ideas from one another and share planning and marketing strategies.

And new products are in the design stage. At the same time, process materials are being created that help hospitals, businesses, social agencies, and schools develop coalitions and become *Champions for Children*®.

This is the right time to champion children

For a host of reasons, educators, in particular, should begin leading the parade to champion children. Two negative forces have combined to create an opportunity – to make this the right time for school people to champion children.

The first negative force

In America, we hold children in low esteem ... or at least we have allowed our actions to produce that perception. All-too-familiar statistics tell us that we should be embarrassed about conditions for children:

> "Never before has one generation of American children been less healthy, less cared for, or less prepared for life than their parents were at the same age," says the National Commission on the Role of the School and Community in Improving Adolescent Health.

> "An anti-child spirit is loose in the land. [America doesn't] even make it into the top ten on any significant indicator of child welfare," writes Sylvia Ann Hewlett in her book, *When the Bough Breaks*.

- This year more than 40,000 American babies will die before their first birthday.

- Every day three children die of injuries inflicted by abusive parents.

- One in five American children lives in poverty – twice the rate for adults.

- Homicide is now the third leading cause of death for all children ages 4-18.

What's doubly upsetting is the fact that these are *familiar* statistics. People know about conditions affecting many of our children, yet, by and large, our society ignores them.

The second negative force

Educators have lost the battle for educational "excellence" in the *nation's* schools, and – perhaps worse – they have been unwilling to admit that selling the public on educational excellence in our *nation's* schools may be a lost cause.

While many of our educational programs and many of our schools *are* excellent, it really doesn't matter. The public isn't buying the notion that our nation has a high quality school system. (About one in five of the people annually surveyed by the Gallup organization give the nation's schools a grade of A or B! And about half believe that the quality of our nation's schools has gotten worse.)

We believe the struggle for excellence was lost on the most strategic of battle grounds — the public mind. Here are three reasons why the battle was lost:

1. The news media out-gunned the education establishment. By producing a continuous flood of articles underlining the short-comings of education and the lack of quality in our schools, the news media have fueled perceptions that are incompatible with the excellence message.

2. Educators advocate every new program as *the* way "to turn things around." This message has created dissonance in the public mind-set. After all, the public reasons — if educators are installing pro-grams to turn things around, they must currently have something that is less than excellent.

3. Business people and their organizations have proclaimed loudly that schools have failed, and educators have not responded to the criticism. One result has been that the business community has suggested a host of school reforms which often are presented in ways that reinforce negative public perceptions of schools.

While we must never give up pursuing excellence and our efforts to improve teaching and learning, it makes sense to abandon proclamations of excellence and redirect those energies to position educators as *Champions for Children®*.

The opportunity

Two negatives — a nation that holds young people in low esteem and our defeat in the battle for educational excellence — give us the opportunity to champion children. After all, educators *are* advocates for children and that's how they are perceived. Now is the time to capitalize on that position to the fullest benefit of our nation's young people. By acting now, educators can do good things, continue the journey toward educational excellence, and increase public understanding of and support for schools.

What do *Champions for Children®* believe?

When people ask what it means to be a *Champion for Children*, you should be able to inspire them with your answer. That's why the following belief statements have become an integral part of the initiative. Use them to answer the question ... or to serve as the foundation for a community dialogue on children ... or to integrate into a board or chamber of commerce resolution.

We are Champions for Children®. We believe in ...

- *providing a safe and secure learning environment for every child*

- *strengthening a healthy, nurturing home life for every child*

- *assuring that every child is loved unconditionally by someone*

- *providing every child with equity of access to quality educational programs and services*

- *nurturing the capacity of every child to pursue a lifetime of learning, thinking, and exploration*

- *developing a society which launches every child into the future equipped with the wisdom — and unencumbered by the liabilities — of previous generations*

- *we believe it is both and honor and a responsibility to reaffirm the worth and dignity of our country's children, to champion their cause, and, through them, to create an enlightened citizenry*

When these belief statements were adopted in New Hampshire, it became apparent that anybody who opposed them probably wouldn't be a strong advocate of young people. This realization encouraged educators to seize the offensive, engage in a Lead Dog marketing strategy, and position themselves as *Champions for Children®*. Who better to lead the parade?

It also became apparent that the responsibility for delivering on these beliefs could not be assigned exclusively to educators. As a consequence, the belief statements were used to build community coalitions. For example, while there are things schools can do to provide a safe and secure learning environment, there are also things that can be done by parents, the business community, the city council, and students themselves. Processing the belief statements provided everyone with an opportunity to step to the mark.

How you can become a *Champion for Children®*

Join forces with those who are involved in the *Champions for Children®* program. By affiliating with the program you'll receive everything you need to get started, including:

- Complete background information on the *Champions for Children®* campaign and a how-to guide to implementing the program;

- Camera-ready copies of the apple logo for your publications and stationery;

- Permission to reproduce the apple logo and words *Champions for Children®* in your publications and stationery;

- Copies of the *Champions for Children®* belief statements to use in building coalitions and alliances for the benefit of children; and,

- Periodic updates on program activities and marketing products to use in your community.

To begin championing children in your community, simply call or write the National School Public Relations Association.

How do you benefit by becoming a *Champion for Children®*?

By championing children, you can capitalize on the opportunity presented by the two negatives. You can lead the crusade to bring people together to focus on our nation's most important resources. You can partner with them to deliver more efficient and effective services to young people, and you can help others understand that educational excellence is a journey for which everyone must take responsibility.

Products that are available (and how you can use them)

NSPRA has developed a number of products to help you communicate the *Champions for Children®* message. There are also products to help you address the needs of young people in your community — and more products and processes are being developed.

(Please note that you do not have to affiliate with the *Champions for Children®* program to purchase *Champions for Children®* products.)

Product	How you can use them
Lapel pin......................	a high-quality way to let others know that you're a *Champion for Children®*. Wear it, use it to enlist others as advocates, or give it as a token of appreciation to others who are *Champions for Children®*.

Posters......................feature the apple logo and proclaim *"We Champion Children Here."* Post them anywhere ... they come in 2 sizes.

Decals......................to use on entrance and office doors ... for schools, for businesses, for anyone who wants to say that *"We Champion Children Here."*

Thank you card........with matching envelope featuring the apple logo on the front of the card and the back flap of the envelope ... for thanking people for anything.

Note pads.................50-sheet, 4" x 5" note pads ... to jot reminders or to send a few encouraging words. They have the apple logo and the words *"Champions for Children"* at the top.

Stickers.....................18 peel-and-stick stickers per sheet, in 3 sizes. Three different sheets to use on stationery, homework, or awards.

Magnets.................. to help children display their papers or to help you post important messages.

Good News notes.. half-sheets to use to send good news about anything.

Friday folders......... indestructible 10" x 13" envelopes with the logo and words *"Champions for Children®."* Use them as a portfolio, to carry projects between home and school, and to store student materials for conferences.

A tip sheet pack........contains practical tips on a variety of topics, including things principals, secretaries, custodians, bus drivers, school board members, and others can do to Champion Children.

Prenatal guide........ If we want every child to come to school ready to learn, we have to start early. This is a guide to the first 9 months of a child's life with information about the changes in mother and her baby. A great gift from schools, hospitals, community agencies, or anyone else who wants to champion the youngest of our children.

Child development guide...................... for preschoolers, ages 6 months to 5 years. It identifies milestones in the growth and development of children. A great gift for preschool parents.

Sitter packet........... the *"Never Alone!"* child sitter envelope contains a guide for sitters, a tablet of forms to leave instructions for sitters, and a sticker for emergency numbers.

You can be part of the future

When people hear about the *Champions for Children*® program, they tend to nod their approval and say, "It's about time. You're right on target." And then they often suggest ways to enhance the program or they talk about the ways they're improving educational opportunities for young people.

NSPRA invites you to be a part of this exciting, proactive program -- to join with others and experience the excitement that comes from sharing new ideas while engaging in activities that mark you and your colleagues as *Champions for Children*®. Simply call or write NSPRA for information.

140

Marketing in action
Taking it personally

Marketing in action
Taking it personally

If it's to be it may be up to ... you!

Pretend for a moment that you are a political consultant. One day someone comes to you seeking advice and counsel. The person wants you to help him run for office, and, during the course of your conversation, tells you he has a 20 percent public confidence rating.

What would you say to this person? If you were honest, you'd say, "People either don't know you, or -- worse yet -- they know you and don't like you. I think you ought to sit this election out while you do some analysis and work to increase your confidence rating. Then, if your confidence rating does improve, consider running four years from now."

Now suppose you receive another visitor to your office. She, too, wants your help in a public campaign. As you talk she tells you that her pollster reports that she has a 65 percent confidence rating. What would you say to this person? Probably something like, "Sit down. Let's talk."

In the annual Gallup/PDK polls of public attitudes toward the public schools, about 20 percent of the respondents give the nation's public schools a grade of A or B. At the same time about twice as many people give "the schools in your community" an A/B rating, and more than three times as many give "the school attended by your oldest child" an A/B confidence rating. Where do you think educators should be spending their marketing dollars?

Well ... you're at least half right! You need to market your school district. It's important to communicate with the people served by the system because marketing the system allows you to leverage your resources and coordinate your efforts.

But everyone in education needs to assume responsibility for marketing. Whether you are a custodian, teacher, secretary, principal, or central office administrator, you need to market yourself, particularly to those who are members of your priority audiences.

The closer schools are to the people and the more personally you communicate with these people, the more effective you are. Here are two key questions you should be asking yourself: What school is closest to the people in my neighborhood? And, who in that school knows people well enough to communicate with them personally?

If you could wave a magic wand and create the ideal school marketing program, it would feature the people in every school -- where public confidence ratings are highest -- communicating as personally as possible with those they serve on a daily basis.

The material which follows was designed to help you create such a Mecca. It begins with a strategy for planning personal development, and moves to a process anyone in any school can use to develop a personal marketing program.

Capitalizing on Change ... Personally

Continuous learning is the key to competitiveness in business. It is the cornerstone of a community's vitality. And it is the foundation of an individual's viability.

If it's true that information is doubling every 18 months ... and that half of what we learn today will be unusable 10 years from now ... and that 90% of today's kindergartners will work in jobs that do not presently exist, then continuous learning is clearly the key to competitiveness, vitality, and viability.

But these things are increasingly personal. They boil down to individuals in a firm or citizens in a community. And when it comes to you, they are the most personal of all.

You need to decide what you need to learn to make you a viable person -- one that contributes to an organization, enhances a community, and has capacity to enjoy "the pursuit of life, liberty, and happiness."

To plan your own program of personal growth, use *The ABC Personal Planner* and follow these steps:

First, write down the mission of your organization. This is the statement that describes the business of your organization -- why it exists. (If no one knows the mission of your organization, draw a little red flag and go to step two.)

Second, write down what you do. If you will, this is a mission statement for you. For example, if you are a teacher and your school's mission is to provide quality programs and services to learners of all ages, then your responsibilities might include being competent in your curriculum area, motivating students to learn, creating an exciting classroom, being an ambassador for the school ... and more. Define what it takes to be the best you can be at the job you have.

Third, identify changes that have potential for impacting you and your organization this year. Look inside *and* outside the organization. But remember that 75-80% of the change that impacts you as an individual is triggered by some external force. That's why you have to have your periscope up, scanning the horizon, anticipating change.

Internally, you might have to accommodate calendar revisions and new staff colleagues, or training opportunities and funding changes. All of these will affect the way you do your job. Externally, new technologies may change the content of your lessons and the way they are delivered. There might be new state mandates, or a new assessment program, or a new competitor.

The point is that we live in a period of radical change and educators do not have special immunity to its implications. The trick is to capitalize on the change. You can start by identifying what you need to learn this year. It's as simple as ABC!

The ABC Personal Planner

The ABCs of continuous learning deserve your continuing attention. Put them in writing. Share them with a colleague or friend. Ask people for their reaction and insights. Then get going. Identify where and when you can get what you need. Finally, put "check up" dates in your calendar every three months. Do your own self-assessment to make sure you're on track. And plan to update the plan and celebrate your successes one year from today.

Today's date _____ My name _____

1. My organization exists to ...

2. It's my job to ...

3. Changes that can impact me

        internally   externally

_____   _____

_____   _____

_____   _____

_____   _____

_____   _____

4. Here is what I need to learn:

   A. to comply with new rules, regulations, mandates, legislation.

   Usually generated by the legal system or legislative bodies, these tend to be things you have to do or accommodate in the performance of your work responsibilities. For example, educators are required to report suspected child abuse. You need to know what to report to whom by when. Odds are you'll learn about such rules, regulations, mandates, and legislation from printed materials or regularly scheduled staff information sessions.

what I need to learn	where	by when
_____	_____	_____
_____	_____	_____
_____	_____	_____

   B. to continuously improve my capacity.

   These are things you need to learn to keep your professional edge. You might need to learn about a new teaching methodology or discoveries and advances in your field or potential applications of technology. You'll tend to learn these things from specific topic training seminars or through a professional association.

what I need to learn	where	by when
_____	_____	_____
_____	_____	_____
_____	_____	_____

C. to position myself to capitalize on change.

This is the risk-taking, entrepreneurial dimension of your learning. Is there a new technology that will enable you to bring new resources to your classroom? Are there ways to network with other teachers of similar subjects ... or with someone in the community? Is there some thing you can learn which will broaden your perspective and position you for new job opportunities? Is there a person, class, or program that will help you develop and implement an idea?

what I need to learn	where	by when
_____	_____	_____
_____	_____	_____
_____	_____	_____

The ABC Personal Marketing Planner

In a marketing relationship, what you have to sell is you.

What are the key characteristics of the environment in which you are functioning?

What are the key changes which have occurred in this environment during the past couple of years?

What are the critical issues facing your organization?

What do you have that people...

need

want

_____ _____

_____ _____

_____ _____

Who are the people who...

    need what you have   want what you have

_____   _____

_____   _____

_____   _____

Profile the people who...

    need what you have   want what you have

_____   _____

_____   _____

_____   _____

Where can I get what you have...

    cheaper   better   more conveniently

_____ _____ _____

_____ _____ _____

_____ _____ _____

What competitive advantages do you have in this marketplace?

What is your position in the marketplace?

Do you want a different position?

What position do you want?

What will you need to do to get the position you want?

What are your personal marketing priorities?

objective A _____

key message _____

target audience:

media:

sequential steps   timeline

_____   _____

_____   _____

objective B _____

key message _____

    target audience:

    media:

    sequential steps   timeline

    _____   _____

    _____   _____

objective C _____

key message _____

    target audience:

    media:

    sequential steps   timeline

    _____   _____

    _____   _____

Marketing in action
School finance campaigns

Marketing in action
School finance campaigns

Here's a salute to those who know how to win school finance elections

Millions of Americans will vote in school elections this year. Not many will stand in the voting booth deciding which lever to pull. Most will have known for a long time.

On election day, personal values motivate people to visit their polling places and express their convictions. They step in the voting booth, close the curtain, and pull one of two levers -- yes or no.

Can school districts influence this personal choice and exercise any control over which lever is pulled? Those who know how to market can.

In fact, you're already influencing the level of support for your school district and the outcome of your next election. If you've ever wondered how you're doing, pause for a moment and check yourself against the ten characteristics of winners -- things successful school districts use to deliver yes votes on election day. If you can integrate these tips into your planning and marketing, odds are good you'll win your next election.

Campaigns don't win elections

Winners understand that campaigns don't win elections. They know that year-round educational marketing programs do.

Campaigns are conducted to harness support that already exists, and support exists where peoples' needs and wants are addressed on a regular basis.

Winners work at the marketing process. They plan every move with the customer in mind, and they believe every communication failure can cost them votes.

Tip 1:

> *The campaign plan must enhance the marketing process, not vice-versa. Put your marketing plan in writing. Make sure your communication is planned, two-way, and year-round. Then design a campaign plan that complements your marketing program.*

Know what's happening

Winners have "marketplace awareness" -- they know what's happening around them. They understand the educational aspirations of their community. They know what people like and don't like, what people do and don't need. And they advocate and implement educational efforts that are in harmony with the citizenry.

Quite simply, winners have a marketing orientation. They respond to people's needs, giving them what they want. If they can't, they thoroughly explain why. (Then they work with people to figure out how they can!)

At election time winners continue their use of surveys. They assess their chances of winning. And then they use the survey results to amplify strengths and take action on weaknesses ... just as they do year-round.

Tip 2:

> *Begin marketing by conducting a community attitudinal survey. Use it to start a dialogue with your customers. As you listen you'll learn about your marketplace, what the people in it need and want, and what they are willing to support at the polls. Winners don't hold elections to find out how people will vote. They know ahead of time.*

Process produces results

Marketing is not buying 500 bumper stickers. Public relations is not writing four newsletters each year. And election success does not come from producing a fact sheet for voters.

Marketing, public relations, and elections are processes. They can have a definite beginning point (when you decide to do something), but they don't have ending points.

A campaign is not a thing or an event. It is an ongoing process which requires the involvement of people. It's complex, it's not easy, and it takes time.

Tip 3:

Process requires people and a plan. Winners involve staff people in the process first. Then they take their campaign to external audiences. And every step of the way they take time to make sure the process is working.

Commitment is king

Winning school districts have a vision, and they are committed to it. They know where they are going and they have the road maps to get them there.

The same dogged determination is demonstrated in commitment to election success. Winning becomes job one because an unsuccessful election can damage morale and dramatically affect the educational program in the classroom. Winners mobilize their resources and do what needs doing to make sure election day ends with a victory party.

Tip 4:

You need a vision before you can expect commitment. Make sure people know where your school district is headed and how the election relates to this direction. Send a signal that says this is the most important thing on the agenda.

Perform in the spotlight

Winners know that they are on-stage all the time. And they understand that the image is the reality -- that what people think is critically important to their election success.

Winners showcase education, beginning at the school board level. Board meetings are open, and they're conducted in a businesslike manner. Priority agenda positions are given to educational matters. Bids and routine items are treated as secondary -- yet important -- matters.

Board members approach the meeting as if people in the audience are potential investors. (At the end of your next school board meeting ask yourself if those in attendance would be impressed enough to buy stock, having just witnessed a meeting of the corporate board.)

A positive, customer-oriented tone, initially set at the school board meeting, exists at all levels of the winning organization. Teachers demonstrate their proficiency in instructional matters. Support staff members understand the value of their contributions and speak favorably about the school district. Everyone is proud to be a part of the winning organization ... and says so.

Tip 5:

> Do all you can to make people in your school district consistent heroes and winners. Help them understand that they are the image of the school district 24 hours of every day. Make them feel good by giving them responsibility, training, praise, and respect.

Organize for execution

Winners develop detailed campaign plans. So do some losers. The difference is that winners know how to execute.

Some winners develop detailed organizational charts; others use a task force approach. It really doesn't matter what the plan looks like on paper. The real test is whether it will function in a high pressure campaign environment.

It doesn't do any good to plan four informational brochures if the print shop can only deliver two. It doesn't do any good to plan election day telephone reminders if the person responsible for callers doesn't recruit.

Tip 6:

> Assign key campaign tasks to "high speed" people -- people who have a track record for getting the job done. Start by putting the campaign in the hands of one person. Give that person the authority and responsibility for the entire campaign.

Facts and logic don't sell

Winning campaigns are customer-oriented. The message is relevant to the voter.

While election facts and financial logic may provide the foundation of the campaign, as election day nears the message must become more emotional in its appeal. Winning campaigns target the hearts and stomachs of voters.

Most people vote yes because somebody asks them to vote yes. They also vote yes because they believe the schools are good or the teachers care or quality schools are "the American way."

Facts and logic, by themselves, rarely sell anything. (Look at all the things you own. Then ask if all your purchasing decisions were rational?) If your campaign literature is a series of statistics, pie charts, and floor plans, you're headed for trouble. These materials have to be translated into language people can understand, and most people don't understand multi-million dollar school budgets.

> ### Tip 7:
>
> *As you develop your campaign message, ask yourself if the average person can understand it. Ask if it's targeted to address the key questions of key audiences. Ask if it will motivate people to get out of their pajamas, get dressed, drive to the polls, and cast a yes vote. The best way to answer these questions is to ask a sampling of people to review your literature before you print 25,000 copies.*

Community involvement pays

Winners know schools do more than serve students in grades kindergarten through twelve. They involve learners of all ages in school programs, and provide services which people in the marketplace need.

In some winning school districts the adult and community education enrollment is double the student population. Others offer a course when there are enough people to fill it. The key is to be responsive. When people are in schools or touched by what schools do, they are more inclined to support them.

Tip 8:

> *Evaluate your community involvement efforts. If you haven't tapped the adult and community education market, reconsider. Get people involved so you can work with them to address their needs. They'll return the favor by taking care of your school district's needs.*

Winners know how to target

Winners don't take their campaign message to everyone. They know who they need at the polls to win, and they target their efforts, aiming at critical audiences. This means some people get more attention than others.

In an election, some people *are* more important than others. The important people are those who will vote, and those who will vote yes are the most important of all.

Winners always say thank you to their supporters. But, having said thanks and issued a reinforcement, they spend most of their time with undecided voters who are leaning toward yes. They spend as little time as possible with no voters.

Tip 9:

> *Know your targets. Develop techniques for thanking the yes voter. Design materials to convince the undecided. Give these people a reason to vote yes. Then get them to the polls on election day.*

It never ends

Election day will eventually come, but the campaign won't end.

Winners set the stage for the next election by conducting a thorough evaluation. They study voter records. The learn who voted and who didn't. And they try to figure out why by looking at gender, length of residence, voting history, and other factors that can provide insights for the next election. And that's just the beginning.

Winners take post-election evaluation information and integrate it into their year-round marketing plan. They take the first step toward winning again by addressing people's needs long before the next election.

Tip 10:

When the election is over, do a complete evaluation. Check the results against your campaign plan. Learn what worked and what didn't.

Au Contraire: Here's to the losers

Every school district is working on its next election right now. Those who aren't are courting defeat. A School District has a comprehensive educational plan. As the plan was being developed, administrators asked two questions about each component:

- Is this educationally sound?

- Will this help us or hurt us at the polls?

They ask these questions subconsciously every day and more formally in quarterly planning sessions. The district hasn't lost an election in 18 years.

Districts that lose elections have unique characteristics, too. Here are some things you don't want to emulate:

❑ If organizations want to create and keep customers, they need to provide what people need and want. In a changing marketplace, customer analysis is more important than ever. In B School District, growth in high technology businesses brought with it new residents who wanted more than the basics. But the ten-year superintendent kept proposing financial issues which supported the fundamentals of the past. The election was a failure, and the superintendent is now working out of state.

❑ Ignoring process is easy to do but difficult to overcome. Many administrators in one state viewed the annual school levy as a one-day event -- an isolated date on the calendar when voters from across the state could let their voices be heard. One year ignoring the election process led to the defeat of more than 80 percent of the levies on the ballot.

❏ Sometimes school people complain that they are spending so much time on the election that there isn't any time for the curriculum. Not true. Schools that are committed to curriculum are on a mission, and this mission dovetails the campaign. When you are working on the curriculum, you need to be working on the election. C School District designed a lighthouse curriculum, but staff members did all their work internally. The election flopped because the district didn't bring people along and citizens didn't understand the rationale for the new curriculum. Now there isn't any money to support the curriculum. Whether you call it electioneering, communication, or common sense, commit to keeping the people with you.

❏ Most business customers are lost because of a negative employee contact. Customers *are* royalty and they expect to be treated with kindness and respect. In D School District, citizens wishing to address the school board must speak from the orchestra pit of the auditorium, addressing the ankles of board members. How do you think these people react when they're asked for money to support their schools?

In E School District, a local school board makes a Christians-lions event out of curriculum reports to the board. Staff members are criticized publicly and rarely shown respect. It's bad manners to dump on the troops, and it's a campaign killer.

❏ One of our former colleagues has been to more election seminars than anyone. His campaign plans are masterpieces -- timelines, charts -- everything is organized and neat. But he has an eight-election losing streak because he spends so much time planning that he doesn't have time to execute. Sometimes campaigns that look good on paper don't work in the real world.

❏ Did you ever try to explain a $40 million school budget to a person with a $27 checkbook balance? Too many districts use reams of paper to describe budget expenditures, state aid fluctuations, property assessment increases, and the like. This approach doesn't work. It's an old advertising saw that you should sell the sizzle, not the steak. In the school business, that means talking about the school program and what it means to people. And, when it comes to money, you need to use numbers people can understand -- dimes per day or dollars per week.

❏ Three-fourths of Americans do not have school-age children. Many school districts use this demographic fact to save money. They only involve parents, and they don't send their newsletters to "nonparents." All year they ignore the bulk of the population. That leads to the bulk of the population being uninvolved and uninformed. They see nothing in the schools for them, and that's reason enough for them to vote no on election day.

❑ Service clubs are important audiences for the campaign message. But if you sell everyone in the audience, you may only get 40 votes from the Kiwanis Club.

While key audiences like this can't be ignored, make sure you have other campaign targets that will help generate the votes you need to win. Add up the number of likely yes voters. Determine if you have enough to win. (See if you can beat the highest no vote ever cast.) E School District discovered -- after four election losses -- that it could have won every election by getting half of the parents of first graders to vote yes. The next campaign was targeted to parents in grades one, two, and three. It passed.

❑ Everything in life seems to run full cycle, yet losers don't close the loop. After a victory F School District didn't do a post-election analysis. They lost their next election as a result. The reason: minority groups carried the successful election because the ballot issue contained something they wanted. This produced a turnout anomaly which wasn't present in the subsequent election.

Election successes are often based on promises. If you win, deliver what you promise. Then close the loop by telling people that you delivered on your promise. Never let people believe that they were misled.

Marketing in action
How to leave a legacy

Marketing in action
How to leave a legacy

William J. Banach speaks to being remembered positively

"It was after midnight when our meeting ended last night. As I drove home, I began to reflect on my 13 years as a school board member -- the ups, the downs, the countless hours. My reflection ended as I pulled into the driveway asking myself, *"I wonder if it's all worth it?"*

The school board member sharing her story with me was expressing what a lot of school board members think, especially after those meetings that drone on and on before ending with too few accomplishments and too many frustrations. The occasion that generated the story was a workshop I was conducting for the Illinois Association of School Boards. Its title: *How to Leave a Legacy.*

I learned a lot during my three-hour workshop, perhaps more than the participants. I learned that school board members -- by and large -- think about doing meaningful things. I learned that their frustration level is high. I learned that they want to be remembered for making a positive contribution -- doing something that is "worth it." And, I reaffirmed that leaving a legacy requires reflective thinking and planning.

In the year since the workshop, I've discovered that wanting to be remembered positively is not unique to school board members. There are a lot of conscientious people giving time to a multitude of worthwhile public and private sector causes who want the same thing. Unfortunately, many of them also are wondering, *"I wonder if it's all worth it?"*

Give Your Organization A Gift

Every school board member worth remembering -- indeed, anyone who works in an organization -- needs to reflect on the realities of the research related to changing a system. Basically this research says that large scale systemic change is very complex and takes a long time.

Too often people who are elected to school boards ignore the reality of this research. They expect the good ship education to make a 90-degree (or 180-degree!) turn overnight. Some really believe that when they get on board, they can change things over the course of a few meetings.

Here's how to recognize the first signs of a school board that is going to turn things around before sunset: A host of special meetings immediately following the school board elections indicate storms ahead. Meetings that drone into the night and all-day Saturday "work sessions" also signal turbulence. These meetings tend to be remembered for their length and the level of frustration among administrators and staff. The focus is on "turning things around," but in the process these meetings often dampen staff initiative, negate years of hard work, and destroy community relations. Listening and learning are low on everyone's agenda. The dialogue is punctuated with remarks like: "One thing I'd like to change around here is ...." "We won't be doing that any longer if I have anything to say about it." "I'm prepared to go to the mat on this." Remarks are characterized by a lot of personal pronouns and tend to pit people against one another. And the focus is usually on what an individual or interest group wants as opposed to what will benefit the system and the learners it serves.

Change research tells us that you can't change a system by focusing on its parts, which is what people in education (and in business!) tend to do. We identify a problem such as low test scores in reading. We then yank reading from the system, study it, change our approach to it, and stuff it back into the system. We forget what systems guru Russell Ackoff tells us — that a system is a function of the interaction of its parts. Put another way, when you change a piece of the system, you affect the entire system. It's virtually impossible to change reading, for example, without regard for other parts of the education system, including teaching methodology, the school schedule, inservice training, and school-community relations.

So, how do you make a difference ... or leave a legacy? You begin by attending to the research, and acknowledging that large scale systemic change *is* complex and *does* take time.

If you rush change, odds are you'll lose more than you gain. And if you order it or legislate it, you'll get foot-dragging or creative compliance that lasts as long as you do.

And that brings us to another point: No matter how intense you are, no matter how good or bad your ideas, no matter how positive or negative your behaviors, the system will out-last you. Whether people say good-bye to you with tears in the eyes or joy in their hearts will depend on the contributions you have made and the ways you have made them. But all this aside, in the end, the system will be there when you're gone.

Actually that was a key premise to my workshop. If you have a dream, I said, odds are you won't see it. Here's why: the typical school board member serves one term or less, which is hardly enough time to effect meaningful change (but plenty of time to cause meaningless disruptions). School staff members are also affected by time. Most change jobs, retire, or otherwise move on before their dream is realized.

As a result, leaving a legacy -- being remembered as someone who made a positive difference -- requires that you give your system two gifts -- the gifts of vision and process.

Vision is the first gift. It speaks to where your organization is headed. It is a written picture of the best that can ever be. It is a destination you'll never reach (because as soon as you get close you'll elevate your vision). It is "the dream." When a vision is embraced by an organization, nothing is a more powerful driver of meaningful change.

Process is the second gift. It's the vehicle an organization can use to engage people and build a constituency as it journeys toward its vision. Process enables the organization to accommodate change and make the continuing mid-course corrections that are a part of every change initiative.

The gifts of vision and process are the best gifts you can give your organization because they're bigger than you are. They'll be there long after you're gone. They are what is takes to change a system. They are, quite simply, keys to leaving a legacy.

Give Yourself A Gift, Too

As I've reflected on my workshop, I have come to realize that there's a third component to being remembered -- a reality that enables you to create and pursue the gifts of vision and process. The third gift is one you give yourself. It's the gift of competence.

All of us are defined by our competence. We say we're pretty good at one thing, but not too hot at something else. We can be a good thinker, but a lousy golfer ... a hard worker, but a mediocre mathematician. We assess our competence all the time. Those around us do, too. They know that we're pretty good or pretty bad or somewhere in between. And, so, leaving a legacy requires that you give yourself a gift, too -- the gift of personal competence.

Regardless of your role or responsibilities, leaving a positive legacy dictates that you work toward being the best that you can be. Whether it's the creativity you bring to teaching, the skill you have in leading people, or the caliber of the questions you ask, what you do and how you're remembered depends on your competency.

Leaving a Legacy

Those who attended my workshop gave me some important insights. They gave me a gift that helped me help them. They clarified my thinking and helped me give them a process for leaving a legacy.

Whether you're a school board member, a superintendent, a parent, or a business person, you, too, can use this gift, this process for leaving a legacy. You can use it personally or within the context of any organization.

At the very least, it requires that you engage in some reflective thinking. In fact, just thinking about the process will provide you with new perspectives.

Step one is to answer the questions and write something in the blanks. Do that and you're on your way to leaving a legacy.

Go farther if you want. Engaging your colleagues in the process is a logical second step -- a step that could lead to improving your entire organization.

So, use the process personally or in your organization. Use it to reflect on the past and to envision the future. Use it to wrap the gifts of competence, vision, and process.

The Legacy Leaving Process

A.   *When my organization becomes the best that it can become,*
     it will be known for ...

    1.

    2.

    (Step A leads to a vision ... for your organization. It also can help
     you think about your mission; i.e., your role or primary purpose
     for being.)

B.   *When I become the best that I can become, I will be known for...*

    1.

    2.

    (This speaks to your vision, and provides some insights into the
     competencies you'll need.)

C.   *The best work-related idea I had in the last year was ...*

    _____

    (If you have trouble writing something on this line, you'll have
     trouble leaving a legacy. Ditto if what you write on the line is known
     only to you.)

D.   *Right now I think this is a great idea:*

    _____

    (See the parentheses under C.)

E.   *Here's what's most exciting about what I do:*

    _____

(You've encountered people who are excited about what they do. They bubble over. They're contagious. You've also encountered their opposites -- the naysayers, the stones, the living dead. Find excitement and fun in what you do. If you can't, think about moving on.)

F.   *I was the driving force behind this important accomplishment last year:*

_____

(Some people and some organizations are all motion and no results. But -- in the end -- something has to happen. What you accomplish *does* matter.)

• *Things will be even better if I can make this happen this year:*

_____

("What have you done for me, lately?" This is a great question in a world with a bumper sticker attention span and an MTV memory.)

G.   *Last year I learned an important lesson from this mistake/failure:*

_____

(We learn more from our failures than our successes. One reason: We keep replaying our mistakes, trying to figure out what went wrong "... so we never do that again." Unfortunately, we don't replay or celebrate our successes so we can learn from them. We usually just move on to the next assignment.)

H.   *I almost stepped in this mine field last year:*

_____

(Politics being what it is, you have to watch where you're walking. Sometimes you need "an eye in the back of your head.")

- *Here a mine field I'd better watch out for this year:*

_____

(Anticipation keeps the train on the track. Keep your eyes and ears open for anything with potential to derail the journey toward the vision.)

I.   *I did two things to improve my competence last year:*

    1.
    2.

(As the saying goes, if you're not getting better, you're probably getting worse. Are you better today than you were yesterday?)

- *This year I can improve my competence by ...*

        1.
        2.

(In what ways will you be better tomorrow than you are today?)

J.   *I'll coach, counsel, or mentor these people this year:*

    1.
    2.

(This is a great gift. You get better when you give it!)

K.   *I'll add these two people to my personal network this year:*
    1.
    2.

(It's what you know *and* who you know. Find the competent thinkers. Talk with them.)

L. *When people think about me, I want them to think about*

1.
2.

(In the world of advertising this is your "position" or identity in the marketplace. It's based on perceptions, and it's really important because *it is* the reality.)

M. *These are the two most critical elements in my personal marketing plan this year:*

1.
2.

(If people don't know about the great things you're doing, you need to get the word out. Even the best products in the world are advertised because today being good isn't good enough.)

N. *The first thing I'm going to do to leave a legacy is ...*

_____

_____

_____

(Now you have to do something to make your legacy leaving plan a reality. Find something positive and doable. Write it down. Then check up on yourself. Revisit your legacy plan in three months, and every three months thereafter. Put the visitation dates in your calendar today.)

Appendixes

Appendix A
The Market-Driven System® forms

The dimensions of greatness

_____ 0 --- 1 --- 2 --- 3 --- 4 --- 5 ---- 6 --- 7 --- 8 --- 9 --- 10

_____ 0 --- 1 --- 2 --- 3 --- 4 --- 5 ---- 6 --- 7 --- 8 --- 9 --- 10

_____ 0 --- 1 --- 2 --- 3 --- 4 --- 5 ---- 6 --- 7 --- 8 --- 9 --- 10

_____ 0 --- 1 --- 2 --- 3 --- 4 --- 5 ---- 6 --- 7 --- 8 --- 9 --- 10

_____ 0 --- 1 --- 2 --- 3 --- 4 --- 5 ---- 6 --- 7 --- 8 --- 9 --- 10

_____ 0 --- 1 --- 2 --- 3 --- 4 --- 5 ---- 6 --- 7 --- 8 --- 9 --- 10

_____ 0 --- 1 --- 2 --- 3 --- 4 --- 5 ---- 6 --- 7 --- 8 --- 9 --- 10

_____ 0 --- 1 --- 2 --- 3 --- 4 --- 5 ---- 6 --- 7 --- 8 --- 9 --- 10

_____ 0 --- 1 --- 2 --- 3 --- 4 --- 5 ---- 6 --- 7 --- 8 --- 9 --- 10

Organizational vision

Here's the Webster definition of vision: 1. Something seen in a dream, trance, or ecstasy; specif: a supernatural appearance that conveys a revelation 2. the act or power of imagination 3. the act or power of seeing.

In The MDS process, a statement of vision is a future-oriented, *written picture* of the best that can be. It defines organizational direction and indicates what the organization will look like when it is functioning at optimum.

An unrestricted, compelling vision opens minds and enables people to see things they haven't seen before. It provides the essential perspective for thinking, planning, and marketing.

[It is our vision] to put a man on the moon by the end of this decade.

Our vision is to be the best entertainment company in America.

It is our vision to provide our customers with unsurpassed quality and service.

Organizational mission

In The MDS process, a mission statement identifies the organization's purpose or primary function. The mission statement is present-oriented; that is, it speaks to what the organization does now.

We can help anyone do everything that has anything to do with communication.

It is our mission to provide quality educational services to learners of all ages, aspirations, and abilities.

Our business is transportation.

We're in the entertainment business.

Goals for organizational leaders

Goal 1   _____

_____

_____

Goal 2   _____

_____

_____

Goal 3   _____

_____

_____

Goal 4   _____

_____

_____

What's wrong, right, and wonderful?

What's wrong and needs to be fixed?

What's okay the way it is and ought to be maintained?

What's wonderful and should be made even better?

Organizational priorities

Priority # _____   _____

                         _____

                         _____

Why should we do this?

Where do we want to be in regard to this priority?

Where are we now in regard to this priority?

What are the barriers / obstacles?

What are the enablers / partnering opportunities?

Organizational objectives

Priority # _____

What are our strategic objectives in relation to this priority?

1. _____

2. _____

3. _____

4. _____

5. _____

Organizational activities

Priority # _____   Objective # _____

Activity	Who	By when	Resources	+/-
_____	_____	_____	_____	____
_____	_____	_____	_____	____
_____	_____	_____	_____	____
_____	_____	_____	_____	____
_____	_____	_____	_____	____
_____	_____	_____	_____	____
_____	_____	_____	_____	____
_____	_____	_____	_____	____
_____	_____	_____	_____	____

Marketable assets

Targets	Needs	Competitive advantage
_____	_____	_____
_____	_____	_____
_____	_____	_____
_____	_____	_____
_____	_____	_____

Targets	Wants	Competitive advantage
_____	_____	_____
_____	_____	_____
_____	_____	_____
_____	_____	_____
_____	_____	_____

The marketing planner

What should we market?	To whom?	Why?	Position?
_____	_____	_____	_____
_____	_____	_____	_____
_____	_____	_____	_____
_____	_____	_____	_____
_____	_____	_____	_____
_____	_____	_____	_____
_____	_____	_____	_____
_____	_____	_____	_____
_____	_____	_____	_____
_____	_____	_____	_____
_____	_____	_____	_____
_____	_____	_____	_____
_____	_____	_____	_____

The marketing mix

	Building Awareness	Developing Understanding	Aligning Interests	Decision
Mass communication	_____	_____	_____	_____
Direct print communication	_____	_____	_____	_____
Small group communication	_____	_____	_____	_____
One-on-one communication	_____	_____	_____	_____

Marketing priorities

Priority # _____   _____

_____

_____

Why should we do this?

Where do we want to be in regard to this priority?

Where are we now in regard to this priority?

What are the barriers / obstacles?

What are the enablers / partnering opportunities?

Strategic marketing objectives

Priority # _____

What are our strategic objectives in relation to this priority?

1. _____

2. _____

3. _____

4. _____

5. _____

Strategic marketing activities

Priority # _____   Objective # _____

Activity	Who	By when	Resources	+/-
_____	___	_____	_____	___
_____	___	_____	_____	___
_____	___	_____	_____	___
_____	___	_____	_____	___
_____	___	_____	_____	___
_____	___	_____	_____	___
_____	___	_____	_____	___
_____	___	_____	_____	___
_____	___	_____	_____	___

Evaluation

What we set out to do	% attainment	Plus / minus factors

Appendix B
Marketing Tools

Marketing Tools
Characteristics of effective school boards

Marketing Tools
School board effectiveness

Self-assessments confirm that most school boards don't function as effective teams. It's no wonder.

First, tradition dictates that the team be composed of lay citizens. There are virtually no other qualifications for membership on the team.

Second, while it's the responsibility of the school board to set policy, most citizens don't give much thought to policy ... until they're elected to the school board.

Third, the learning environment of board members is an obstacle to team development. Board members usually come together for two or three hours in a relatively formal setting (the board meeting) once or twice each month. "We have a big agenda tonight," says the chair, "so let's get down to business." Asking questions -- trying to learn -- in this environment can be perceived as a sign of naivete or, over time, stupidity.

Adding board member turnover to the mix exacerbates the problem. Just when the school district becomes blessed with a knowledgeable, fully functioning board team, someone leaves. Then the whole process of board development and team building has to begin anew.

So, how can school board members learn the ropes and come together as a policy-making team? Members of the board must have a concept of what a board should do (a sense of purpose) and a mental picture of what a good school board looks like when it does those things (a sense of vision). Simply putting in seat time at school board meetings does not assure either the purpose or the vision.

The following exercise can provide a starting point for improving the effectiveness of a school board team. First, have each school board member write what he or she believes are the dimensions (or characteristics) of a truly great school board. (Use the "Dimensions of greatness-" form in Appendix A.)

Next, each board member should rate the board on each characteristic that he/she identifies. Use a zero-to-ten scale (zero is low; ten is high). For example, one board member might write that a truly great school board "conducts its work in a businesslike manner," and rate the board a five on that dimension or characteristic.

Next, have every board member rate the board on the characteristics of winning board teams (again using a zero-to-ten rating scale). Then compare the lists and ratings. And, then, have some honest dialogue about what -- if anything -- needs to change.

The characteristics of effective board teams

▌ **Vision and purpose** -- Board members have a vision of the future and they are resolved to work toward it.

    Rate your school board   0 - 1 -2 - 3 - 4 - 5 - 6 - 7 - 8 - 9 - 10

▌ **Goal driven** -- Board members have written goals for the Board. The goals are to move them in the direction of their vision.

    Rate your school board   0 - 1 -2 - 3 - 4 - 5 - 6 - 7 - 8 - 9 - 10

▌ **Results orientation** -- Board members make attainment of goals a priority.

    Rate your school board   0 - 1 -2 - 3 - 4 - 5 - 6 - 7 - 8 - 9 - 10

▌ **Commitment and exhilaration** -- Board members have a deep sense of commitment to their vision and are excited about pursuing it.

    Rate your school board   0 - 1 -2 - 3 - 4 - 5 - 6 - 7 - 8 - 9 - 10

▌ **Sense of togetherness** -- Board members know (and capitalize on) one another's strengths. They tend to say *we* instead of *they*.

    Rate your school board   0 - 1 -2 - 3 - 4 - 5 - 6 - 7 - 8 - 9 - 10

■ **Free-flowing communication** -- Board members have easy access to decision-making information.

Rate your school board   0 - 1 -2 - 3 - 4 - 5 - 6 - 7 - 8 - 9 - 10

■ **Uncompromising quality** -- Board members have high expectations; they dislike doing things that they can't do well.

Rate your school board   0 - 1 -2 - 3 - 4 - 5 - 6 - 7 - 8 - 9 - 10

■ **Inspired leaders** -- Board members perceive themselves as high principle, big picture, future focused, can-do leaders.

Rate your school board   0 - 1 -2 - 3 - 4 - 5 - 6 - 7 - 8 - 9 - 10

■ **External backing** -- The Board's constituency provides support for its vision, mission, and priorities.

Rate your school board   0 - 1 -2 - 3 - 4 - 5 - 6 - 7 - 8 - 9 - 10

■ **Leadership support** -- Board members support the superintendent ... privately, publicly, and professionally.

Rate your school board   0 - 1 -2 - 3 - 4 - 5 - 6 - 7 - 8 - 9 - 10

■ **Political savvy** -- Board members tend not to shoot anyone in the foot, including themselves.

Rate your school board   0 - 1 -2 - 3 - 4 - 5 - 6 - 7 - 8 - 9 - 10

The school board's role in marketing schools

Sometimes school board members wonder why public schools should be concerned about marketing. After all, attendance is compulsory, schools have a ready market, and there isn't any profit motive.

But every school district faces competition of some kind. Some districts compete for students with private or parochial schools. Others compete with home schools. And all districts compete with the allure of the electronic media and the apathy which can lead to inferior academic performance, absenteeism, and -- ultimately -- dropping out.

Even if the need to overcome competition is disregarded, marketing is a natural ally of continuous school improvement. Effective marketing improves everything it touches -- the individual schools, the school district, and the school board.

Because learning is a process, it's dependent on mutually beneficial collaboration between the school district and its clientele. One could say that marketing is the lubricant of mutually beneficial collaboration.

Schools have owners -- taxpayers -- who have expectations. Schools also have clients -- learners -- with needs to be filled. Effective marketing programs can help schools define these expectations and address student needs.

The eroding monopoly

Some critics have said that public schools are not as effective as they could be because "... they are monopolies." (We have been conditioned to believe that there is something inherently bad about monopolies. But most state law enforcement agencies and local fire departments are monopolies in the same sense as the public schools, and they seem to serve the public interest quite well. In fact, there are some who believe the breakup of some monopolies -- most notably the phone companies -- has been a public interest disaster. At the very least it has resulted in nonstop telephone calls, commercials, and direct mail pieces haranguing us to switch services.)

In the past, public schools didn't have a profit motive. In fact, improved performance rarely led to increased revenue or other performance rewards common in the private sector.* But the public school monopoly is eroding, and funding is shifting to a performance base.

---

* On occasion, increased performance has been penalized in the legislative process! When extra funds are taken from the educational pot for poor performing schools, there is less money available for high performing schools. And it's still not uncommon for low performing schools to receive extra funds or grant monies to help them improve their performance. Rarely, if ever, does one hear of high performing schools receiving special appropriations designed to maintain or improve their performance.

More states are adopting "body count" funding formulas which provide a certain amount of money per child. Gain students and revenue increases. Lose students and revenue declines. This is a new twist on the private sector profit motive.

Many states have also introduced "accountability" measures. Initiatives have been introduced to correct substandard performance. And when performance doesn't improve, steps are taken to take control of the school district's educational program.

But there are even more powerful forces operating in the new marketplace. Now there are a host of educational options (public school, private school, parochial school, home school, corporate learning centers, self-instructional materials, distance learning, interactive television, virtual schools, etc.). As the options become more and more viable for consumers, expect a parallel track of changing legislation which makes money available to support a host of consumer choices.

There is a new bottom line for education. The monopoly is eroding. As it does, watch for more emphasis on accountability, emergence of a profit motive, and more money to support those who exercise their educational options.

The focus of marketing

The individual school building is where "the pencil meets the paper." That's where the vast majority of school services are delivered to clients, and it's the natural place to focus marketing efforts.

While the word marketing doesn't appear in a school principal's typical job description, effective marketing is an implied responsibility in every principal's job. Every principal needs to address taxpayer expectations and the needs of learners. This often means that a big part of the principal's job is to make the school user-friendly and responsive to the needs of those it serves.

The same holds true for the superintendent and administrators in central office. While they may not be directly involved in the delivery of instructional services, they do have important contacts with constituents that affect school marketability. How these people do their jobs affects the way that principals and teachers do their jobs.

School boards also function within this marketing arena. Marketing enables boards to provide a framework for planning across the district. Board members need to understand that marketing takes place whether or not there's a marketing plan, and even planned marketing activities can and do occur without the school board's involvement. The school board's involvement in setting the tone is often the difference between good and bad marketing programs.

At the same time, marketing from a districtwide perspective creates obligations for the school board. For example, the results of marketing research often challenge board members to go back to the basics and examine the board's relationship with members of the community.

In short, the outcome of a marketing program depends heavily on the school board. An effective board can do a great deal to insure success by providing credible leadership, setting a positive tone, and modeling professional behavior. Unfortunately, an ineffective board can do the opposite.

Where does the school board fit in?

School boards can contribute to overall marketing success in at least four ways:

1. by establishing and maintaining credibility as the school district's policy-maker and overseer;

2. by articulating the purposes of the schools -- by telling people about the district's vision, mission, and priorities;

3. by supporting district-level marketing services for individual schools and the district; and,

4. by monitoring school district performance in relation to the district's vision, mission, priorities, and marketing initiatives.

The aim of marketing is to provide quality services in such a way that people *want* to do business with the school district. To address this continuing challenge, the school board team needs to ask if people in the district seem eager to do business with the *school board*.

To market your school board, you need to understand that ...

 • It's the board's role to set policy, but the line between policy and procedure can get fuzzy. That's why school board members need to keep asking, "What's this got to do with policy?" Superintendents need to ask the same question. And both school board members and superintendents need to agree that it's okay -- in fact, desirable -- to alert one another to activities which are outside one's role.

 • Vision, mission, and priorities are the domain of the school board and superintendent ... but it's foolhardy to develop these things in isolation. Too many school districts have allowed school improvement teams or other groups to develop district direction and purpose. Wrong. School improvement teams exist to improve teaching and learning. Any vision, mission, and priorities they develop should relate to teaching and learning, and should be developed within the context of the school district's vision, mission, and priorities.

The school board and superintendent must be concerned with the entire school district -- "the big picture." They need priorities which range from curriculum to transportation, from maintenance to budgeting, from alternative programming to staff development. (When a school improvement team or other interest group takes over vision, mission, and priorities, the focus tends to be rather narrow. For example, most school improvement teams don't have priorities related to long-range financial management, facility maintenance, support staff training, community relations, and other topical areas which must be addressed by a school district.)

School district vision, mission, and priorities are big picture concerns. Before developing them, it's wise to engage staff and community (for example, by using The Market-Driven System® and/or by conducting surveys, reviewing community demographics, assessing community support, and conducting community listening sessions).

 • Being prepared makes everyone on the board look good. Remember, the perception *is* the reality. If the first sound after the gavel is board members opening their informational packets, it's a good bet the meeting will not be one in which your best foot is forward.

- *How* boards conduct their business is as important as the business that they conduct. Public confidence should increase as people observe you in action. If your board meetings are the hottest program on cable TV, seek help.

- Preparation, discussion, and honesty often lead to consensus. It takes hard work to understand the full range of issues and agenda items facing a school district. When board members take action based on informed consensus, they need to explain what was involved in their decision-making process; e.g., that the item was initiated and reviewed by a committee or task force, that the various components of the item have been researched during the past six months, that the action was taken following public hearings, etc.

Yet, despite the hard work and the explanations, narrow-minded people sometimes say that board members are "rubber stamps." There's nothing wrong with individual board members expressing opposing opinions, of course. And there's nothing wrong with being on the minority side of a vote. It's when opposing opinions are expressed and negative votes are cast simply to avoid the rubber stamp label that they become disruptive.

- Asking questions is okay. Sincere questions demonstrate that you want to learn. Most school board members -- even those who knew everything on the night of their first school board meeting -- will tell you that it took a year or more before they felt informed about educational matters and comfortable with the responsibilities of being a board member.

- School boards are responsible to *all* the people in their community ... and *all* the students, too. Every decision about every item must be made with the interests of everyone in mind.

School districts are often called school *systems*. People who study systems tell us that a system is " ... a product of the interdependence of its parts." That is, you can't attend to any part of the system without affecting every other part of the system and, indeed, the system itself.

You can't satisfy the athletic supporters without affecting the band boosters. You can't emphasize the arts without affecting the basics. And you can't improve staff development without impacting the budget. Everything is interrelated. People who do not serve on boards find this difficult to understand.

- <u>Every issue is special</u>, even when it's not special to you. When people address the school district through employees or members of the school board, they are expressing something of special interest to them. Even if it's not important to you, it's important to them ... and they will judge you by the courtesy and skill with which you respond.

- <u>Board members are simply citizens until there's a quorum and the meeting is called to order.</u> Unless it's an official board meeting, everything an individual board member does is unofficial. The school district is not well served by school board members who play the Lone Ranger or Rambo.

- <u>It's important to have a board "understanding."</u> Understand how your board "does business." Know what is expected of committee chairs ... what to do when you're uncertain ... who speaks for the board, etc. When things are going well these things aren't important. But guess what? Lack of attention to these things can derail a board, and when things start going downhill these are the things that get really important. Deal with them now.

- <u>School board members are targets.</u> People try to pick them off, one at a time. If people are calling you, they're also calling some or all of your colleagues. Make sure you know about those board "understandings." Listen to people, tell them how your school board does business, and steer them to the people who should be helping them.

- <u>When a majority of the board votes to support A, it's time to stop lobbying for B.</u> In a democratic society, the majority rules. There is dialog and debate, and then a vote. The vote determines outcome and direction. Those who can't shift their thinking to the next discussion undermine the democratic process.

- <u>Executive sessions are permitted by law so that certain matters can be discussed in confidence.</u> Leaking confidential information is a violation of the public trust ... and generally disgusting behavior. Enough said.

- <u>When school board members play "stump the stars," everyone looks bad.</u> Ambushes and sniping are terrorist techniques, and surprises should be saved for birthdays. Teachers, administrators, and other staff members are usually on the school board agenda to inform or to enhance board member understanding, not to be embarrassed or "raked over the coals."

* <u>Being visible is important.</u> When board members attend school events and district activities, people notice. Show up ... look presentable ... be informed ... and emulate sponges. You can share what you "soak up" with your board colleagues at the next meeting.

* <u>Communication means different things to different people.</u> Sometimes people say, "You didn't communicate" when they really mean, "I didn't get my way." Do let people blame things on "poor communication." When things go wrong, it's usually the result of the way you do business or how people get treated in the process. When people say that there has been a communication breakdown, do some serious thinking about what they really mean.

People have varying degrees of confidence in their school boards. Some have a great deal; others have very little. Most are somewhere between the extremes (and most of these boards are on the positive side of the continuum).

Boards that generate confidence project an image of professionalism, fairness, and efficiency. This isn't always easy for a governmental body that's designed to provide popular control of a public institution. Public accountability keeps the school board in the middle of a political arena where rewards and sanctions sometimes detract from the positive characteristics most school boards possess.

Moreover, without consensus on how to judge performance, schools depend on rules and regulations to ensure accountability. And those rules and regulations can create a bureaucracy which stifles creativity and individual initiative at the building level.

Board members who are interested in effective marketing begin with a thorough self-evaluation. Then they help remove the obstacles that people encounter when they communicate with the school district. If you're committed to improving school board performance, start by using the self-assessment sections of The Market-Driven System®. In some states, school board and administrator associations and regional education organizations are available to lend a hand facilitating or providing some "outside insight."

Marketing Tools
Sample dimensions of greatness

Marketing Tools
Sample dimensions of greatness

The MDS process begins with participants identifying the dimensions (or attributes or characteristics) of a truly great school district (or school or department).

The exercise is designed to help people think about the kind of school district they'd like to have and to assess themselves against it. The exercise also improves communication and understanding because it helps participants learn one another's educational priorities. In fact, one could say that the exercise identifies what people value in their school district.

The Dimensions of Greatness which follow were identified by people who have participated in The MDS process. The list should provide you with a sense of what to expect from this exercise. You can also use some of the dimensions as examples when you explain this exercise in your school district.

- A sense of vision and mission
- Open access to decision-making information
- Free and open exchange of ideas
- Community involvement
- High expectations for everyone

- A stimulating climate for teaching and learning
- Access to technology
- A climate of openness, honesty, and trust
- A future-focused curriculum
- Students who are excited about learning

- Teamwork between departments
- Student-teacher-administrator cooperation
- Administrative support
- Staff commitment to life-long learning
- Participatory decision-making processes

- A student-centered learning environment
- A results-oriented staff
- Safe/secure learning environment
- Diversity of program
- Free and open exchange of ideas

- An effective staff development program
- Ongoing processes to monitor effectiveness
- School-community partnerships
- Entrepreneurial spirit
- High educational standards

- A collegial environment
- A community that supports learning
- Motivated, enthusiastic students
- Adequate financial resources
- An environment where everyone is learning

Marketing Tools
Sample vision statements

Marketing Tools
Sample vision statements

Vision statements provide a written picture of an organization's destination. They are future-focused statements that center on what we want. We like to say that they describe your school district functioning at optimum.

Vision statements can be as short as one sentence or somewhat more elaborate. These vision statements were developed by people who have participated in The MDS process.

Sample 1

It is our vision to create a school district which prepares all learners for the future.

Sample 2

Our vision is to create a student-focused school system which is acknowledged for the caliber of its thinking, the quality of its staff, and the competence of its graduates.

The school district we envision ...

- *creates enthusiasm for learning*
- *nurtures intelligent risk-taking*
- *develops an appreciation for life-long learning*
- *helps students assume responsibility*
- *includes parents and community members as partners in the learning process*

Sample 3

It is the vision of _____High School to be a comprehensive learning center which serves all people in the community.

In pursuit of this vision, _____ High School will ...

- *focus on student achievement and success*

- *create forums for continuing interaction with the community*

- *be a place where people are excited about learning*

Sample 4

Our vision is to create an exemplary school district which is acknowledged for the caliber of its graduates, the quality of its staff, and the diversity of its program.

The school district we envision ...

- *creates enthusiasm for learning*

- *nurtures intelligent risk-taking and bold experimentation*

- *is characterized by openness and trust*

- *capitalized on change*

- *functions as a showcase for the possible*

Marketing Tools
Sample mission statements

Marketing Tools
Sample mission statements

Mission statements describe an organization's reason for being. They are present-oriented statements that describe what the organization does.

As is the case with vision statements, mission statements can be as short as one sentence or somewhat more elaborate. These mission statements were developed by people who have participated in The MDS process.

Sample 1

It is our mission to engage learners of all ages in a comprehensive educational process which helps them ...

- *think clearly*
- *communicate effectively*
- *capitalize on change*
- *assume responsibility*
- *learn continuously*
- *prepare for their future*

Sample 2

It is the mission of the _____ School District to provide educational opportunities which enable students of all aspirations and abilities to develop their full potential.

In pursuit of this mission, the _____ School District will ...

- *maintain a learning environment characterized by academic achievement and independent thought*

- *strengthen school-community partnerships*

Sample 3

It is the mission of _____ High School to prepare students for the future by providing them with a foundation for continuous learning.

In pursuit of this mission, _____ High School will ...

- *model enthusiasm for thinking, learning, and doing*

- *provide a comprehensive curriculum*

- *create an environment of mutual respect and high expectations*

- *engage the community*

- *teach students to enjoy responsibility*

Marketing Tools
Sample priority statements

Marketing Tools
Sample priority statements

Sample school board priorities

In The MDS process school board members define their role as a school board and adopt priorities for themselves. This helps board members keep their policy focus while reaffirming their support for the planning process.

School board members typically adopt 3 - 5 priorities (or goals) for themselves. Here's a sample:

The role of the _____ School Board is to develop policy and provide support for school district employees as they fulfill their responsibilities to the constituents of the _____ Community School District.

To address its role, the _____ School Board has adopted these goals for itself:

1. To establish forums in which there can be more discussions of substance on educational matters.

2. To initiate collaborative relationships which benefit the educational process.

3. To improve school board communication, particularly as it relates to helping citizens understand the school board's decision-making process.

4. To participate in learning opportunities which strengthen the capacity of the School Board.

5. To develop a process for following up on new programs and educational initiatives.

Sample school / department priorities

In The MDS process teams from each building and department come together to plan. An important part of that planning is to identify one districtwide priority and up to three building or department priorities.

Here are sample priority statements adopted by teams participating in The MDS process:

_____ High School

Districtwide priority:

■ to facilitate the change process at the building level by creating forums in which schools can plan cooperatively

School priorities:

■ to create an environment in which students can build ownership in and take responsibility for their education

■ to enhance _____ School's linkages to the external community (e.g., to such concerns as business and institutions of higher education, and through such vehicles as apprenticeships and information technology)

■ to develop a flexible school schedule in which constraints such as time, class size, and the unavailability of technology are minimized

_____ High School

Districtwide priority:

- ■ To create a sense of purpose and collective responsibility within the school-community

School priorities:

- ■ To develop a process which enhances community understanding of and appreciation for diversity

- ■ To create a school environment which enhances respect for self and others

- ■ To establish quality standards for students and staff

_____ School

Districtwide priority:

- ■ to develop processes which enable school employees to understand and address customer needs

School priorities:

- ■ to speed the pace with which technology is being integrated into instructional and administrative tasks

- ■ to provide training which focuses on the management of change in all staff responsibility areas

- ■ to inventory and develop plans for addressing the needs of individual students

_____ School

Districtwide priority:

▮ to improve internal and external communication and involvement

School priorities:

▮ to develop plans for evaluation and articulation of the curriculum

▮ to develop a model for a school-centered learning community

▮ to develop a collaborative model of communicating with staff, students, parents, and other members of the community

_____ School

Districtwide priority:

• To create time for professional sharing and collaboration

School priorities:

• To create time for professional sharing and collaboration

• To develop an awareness of and appreciation for diversity

Business Department

Districtwide priority:

- To develop a participative management system characterized by openness, trust, commitment, and accountability

Business Department priorities:

- To design and implement a program of self-directed and self-managed teams

- To provide Business Department employees customer relations training

- To better relate Business Department roles and functions to the nature and schedule of work

Maintenance/Grounds Department

Districtwide priority:

- To provide school district employees with training in the area of public relations

Maintenance/Grounds Department priorities:

- To design and implement a team-building program

- To develop a year-round plan for the maintenance of school district equipment

Transportation Department

Districtwide priority:

- ▮ To help employees of the school district become more sensitive to the needs of the people they serve

Transportation Department priorities:

- ▮ To improve communication with one another

- ▮ To provide training and support to help bus driver improve their client relations

- ▮ To involve drivers in the planning of routes

Sample school district priorities

In The MDS process school district priorities "bubble up" from the priorities of the buildings and departments. In the end, they are the result of all the work of all the people who have been involved in The MDS process.

Typically, there are 4 - 6 priorities at the district level. Here are sample priority statements adopted by districts participating in The MDS process:

■ *To streamline operational procedures*

■ *To design and implement a comprehensive staff development program*

■ *To improve internal and external communication*

■ *To develop an ongoing assessment of curriculum, teaching, and learning*

■ *To enhance the school district's outreach programming*

■ *To develop a customer orientation*

■ *To nurture and reward vision-related risk-taking*

■ *To develop a process for regularly obtaining community and staff feedback*

Marketing Tools
Getting representative feedback

Marketing Tools
Getting representative feedback

On the next few pages, we'll give you an overview of several tools that you can use to gather opinions and attitudes from people in your community. We'll discuss citizen committees, focus groups, and surveys, briefly mentioning several suggestions for each technique. Then we'll focus more directly on surveys, offering you more in-depth information about why and how to use them.

Citizen advisory committees

Someone once said that the best committee has five members, four of whom are home sick. There's an important message in this gallows humor: Limit committee membership or organize the committee into task-groups so those who serve aren't immobilized by the size of the group.

Citizen advisory committees can do two things simultaneously: First, they can serve as a vehicle for meaningfully involving people in the schools. And, second, they can provide valuable feedback from the constituents of your school district.

When you form a citizen advisory committee, know what you want the committee to do. Then communicate that clearly to all who serve. Tell them why they were selected to participate. And then tell them that they are serving in an *advisory* capacity -- that the information they generate will be used in the district's decision-making process. Underline the advisory nature of the committee by telling members when their assignment ends.

For example, tell committee members that they are being asked to spend four months assessing the facility needs of the school district. Tell them the purpose of the study is to provide information which the school board can use in its facility planning. Then tell the committee members their assignment will begin on September 1st and end on December 31. On that date -- tell them so there can be no misunderstanding! -- the committee will be disbanded.

■ **Strengths**

Citizens advisory committees are particularly effective when they're formed for a specific task. A committee can also open an ongoing dialogue with citizens, allowing you to explore the best thinking of individuals who have special interests and abilities.

■ **Weaknesses**

Committees must be relatively small to be effective. But the smaller the committee, the less representative the feedback will be, unless you select members to represent all interest groups. Another drawback is that committee members might misunderstand their purpose or limitations, and take off on tangents or -- heaven forbid -- begin to believe they are the school board.

■ **Suggestions**

Give members written guidelines on goals, purposes, and procedures to keep them on track. Tell them whether they are to draft goals, give input to a goal-writing process, or react to the goals that the professional staff drafts. Tell them if your school board is seeking information, advice, or both.

- ■ Clarify the advisory role of the committee. Its job is to recommend, not decide. The school board must eventually be satisfied that committee recommendations are consistent with the school district's vision, mission, and goals.

- ■ Make the membership representative of your community -- racially, socially, economically, and politically. Don't cater to those who have a one-issue agenda; instead, impanel people with differing points of view to avoid rubber-stamp perceptions.

- ■ Provide members with background information, speakers, films, and other resources to enhance their discussions.

Because the primary function of a broad-based citizens' committee is to help your district refine its sense of direction, community members must know what's going on. Citizens need to know about the nature of the committee's discussions, the committee's recommendations, the rationale for them, and the action that will be taken. Keeping the process under wraps obscures the committees' purpose and the citizen involvement your district is trying to develop.

Focus groups

Focus groups are designed to provide in-depth information about a specific topic. Their purpose is to zero-in (or *focus*) on a single subject, such as communication, community education programming, school priorities, or a bond issue strategy.

Typically, 8-10 people are invited to spend 90-minutes in a structured group interview, telling you what they think about the topic under consideration.

■ **Strengths**

Focus groups provide a structured way to gather in-depth information on a given subject.

Focus groups can involve people with a common interest (such as local merchants or band boosters or pre-school parents) or people who are hand-picked because of their interest or knowledge of the subject you're investigating.

The dynamics of the group produce a synergistic effect; i.e., the moderator and the participants all stimulate the dialogue.

Focus groups can generate information quickly and at a reasonable cost.

■ **Weaknesses**

Only a limited number of people can be involved in any one focus group (but you can conduct more than one focus group on a single subject).

The information generated during the focus group is qualitative and, hence, sometimes difficult to interpret.

Focus groups require a skilled moderator.

▌ Suggestions

Focus groups can range from highly organized, videotaped sessions to very informal conversations.

Focus group moderators must be effective at directing an unbiased, relaxed discussion. Jeanne Magmer, a past president of the National School Public Relations Association, offers these suggestions:

▪ Limit the size of your focus groups to about 10 people. Larger groups don't allow everyone a chance to talk.

▪ If you want to increase the number of people you are involving in your project, increase the number of focus groups you use.

▪ Limit the length of the focus group sessions from 60 to 90 minutes.

▪ Limit the number of subjects to three or four.

▪ Ask only open-ended questions. For instance, you might ask what the school district does well, or what problems the district faces. Ask the group to consider these questions as a starting point or as a guide to their discussion. Remember that the best insights and ideas spring from no-holds-barred dialogue.

▪ Begin on a positive note to place the problems and the discussion into proper perspective. End the same way.

▪ Know who is going to compile and interpret the findings from the focus group -- and know ahead of time how you'll use that information. For instance, will the board use the information, will an internal staff committee use it, or will a citizen committee use it?

Surveys

Surveys are designed to obtain representative data from a population (or universe) whose size makes it impossible or impractical to interview every person. For example, it's probably impossible and certainly impractical to interview 50,000 registered voters in a community.

Surveys allow you to select samples that represent a population. From these samples you can project how the entire population would have answered the questions had all the members of the population been interviewed.

Surveys are decision-making tools. Responses to a questionnaire need to be analyzed and interpreted. Then the knowledge gained should be used to enhance the decision-making process.

▋ Strengths

Surveys can provide *representative* feedback. They provide a more realistic perspective than "two calls to a school board member" or a special interest group claiming "everyone" wants -- or doesn't want -- what ever.

Surveys are fast. A properly designed survey can be done quickly. A telephone survey, for example, can be conducted over the course of one or two evenings.

Surveys are accurate. Properly designed surveys enable you to talk about the results you obtain with predetermined levels of confidence.

Surveys are relatively inexpensive. While it is possible to spend a great deal of time and money on surveys, most school surveys -- particularly written and telephone surveys -- are relatively inexpensive.

▋ Weaknesses

You can't learn everything you want to know by conducting a survey. (Indeed, it's a common survey mistake to try "to find out everything.") Surveys need to be focused, and then they need to be followed by analysis and, perhaps, further investigation in the form of another survey or a focus group.

People who respond to school surveys have varying degrees of interest and knowledge. That's why they are referred to as *opinion* polls. For example, taxpayers may not have any idea of the costs of education. That's why they often support having computers in every classroom but scream foul when you ask for the money to buy them (let alone the software and teaching training).

Surveys provide snapshots in time. They reflect public opinion at the time they are taken. You shouldn't be basing your strategic plan on a survey which was conducted two or three years ago.

■ **Suggestions**

Before conducting a survey, know what you want to know. Do you want to gather demographic information such as the ages and occupations of residents? (You may be able to obtain this information without doing a survey!) Or, do you want to find out what people do and don't like, or are you interested in the priorities they have for their schools?

Surveys are *not* decision-makers. Promising people that you will do "whatever the survey says" is courting disaster. What will you do if half the people favor something and the other half don't? What will you do if 49 percent of the people like your idea while 51 percent oppose it? Using a survey to make decisions for you is a mistake. At the very least it's abdication of leadership responsibility.

12 reasons you should conduct surveys

Here are a dozen reasons for conducting a survey:

■ *To find out how effectively you're communicating.* Do people really feel well-informed about your schools? Where do they get their information? Which information sources do they trust? Which don't they trust? What thoughts do they have for improving communication?

■ *To learn how people feel about athletics.* Do they want to increase the number of athletic teams? For both males and females? Do they support intramural programming? Should fitness and life-long sports be emphasized more than competitive sports?

■ *To assess staff morale in your schools.* What do people like about their jobs? What don't they like? What ideas do they have for improving the way things are done? What kinds of training would they like?

■ *To determine what the people in your community expect from the schools.* Do they want you to focus on the college-bound? Should you place more emphasis on the school-to-work transition? Should you hold the line on new programs?

■ *To learn if high school students feel that they are receiving adequate preparation for the future.* How satisfied are they with career counseling? Do they think their courses are preparing them for the future? How do students who graduated three years ago feel about the schools?

■ *To determine if citizens want to be more involved in their schools.* What is the nature of the involvement they want"? How can you encourage them to volunteer?

■ *To assess the adult or continuing education market.* Are people in the community interested in taking classes in your schools? What classes do they want? How much are they willing to pay? What times of the day and which days of the week are most convenient for them?

■ *To find out if your bond issue is likely to pass.* Are people getting the information they need to make a decision? What are the opinion leaders saying about the issue? What has people confused?

■ *To determine the perceived health of the school district.* All things considered, what grade would people give you for the job you're doing? Why? What goals would they set for your schools?

- *To learn the viewpoints of those who don't have school-age children.* Do they really care about the schools? What is it that these "nonparents" want to know?

- *To discover how much support there is in the business community.* What does the business community think about your graduates? How would the business community like to be involved in your schools? What could business people do to enhance the educational process?

- *To determine the critical issues facing your schools.* Do most people identify the same issues? What are their ideas for resolving the issues?

Whether your intent is to start a new program, promote a bond issue, revamp your communication program, or simply "get a handle" on what people in your community are thinking, you need to consider using a survey.

Excuses that people use for *not* conducting surveys

Some people are afraid of what they might learn from a survey. So, in effect, they stick their heads in the proverbial sand and hope that whatever is out there is either okay or will go away. Even someone with casual knowledge of public institutions knows this is a strategy for disaster.

Despite this, some school people don't want to know what people are thinking. Other people don't trust samples. (They're the people who want to "mail the questionnaire to everybody" or "put a copy of the questionnaire in the newspaper.") They don't understand the statistics of sampling and the fact that samples can provide an accurate and representative picture of public perceptions.

These people need to understand how people – including them – use samples every day. For example, if Dad is making 5 gallons of his secret chili, he doesn't have to eat it all to determine if it tastes the way it should. He stirs the pot and tries a spoonful now and then. Similarly, when the doctor orders a blood test, the technician doesn't drain all your blood. A small amount – a sample – is taken from your arm or finger tip.

Other people don't use surveys because they believe that the survey process is too complicated. But surveys are largely a matter of logistics once the questionnaire is developed.

Then there are those who believe they'll have trouble managing all the logistical details that are associated with surveys. That's why a planning calendar is essential.

Surveys: The essential steps

We believe that there are 18 essential steps in any survey research project:

1. Decide what you want to learn from the survey.
2. Determine if you can get this information without doing a survey.
3. Determine the target audience for the survey.
4. Determine the type of survey method you'll use.
5. Decide how accurate you want your survey results to be.
6. Develop a timeline for the survey project.
7. List the resources you need to do the survey.
8. Draw the sample.
9. Outline the content areas of the survey and write the first-draft questions.
10. Refine the question wording and design the questionnaire format.
11. Pretest the draft questionnaire.
12. Use the pretest findings to develop the final questionnaire.
13. Recruit and train interviewers.
14. Conduct the interviews or administer the written surveys.
15. Tabulate the data.
16. Analyze the results
17. Report the new knowledge.
18. Use the results

You'll find everything you need to know about surveys in *The ABC Complete Book of School Surveys*.

Marketing Tools
Sample survey questions

Marketing Tools
Sample survey questions

These sample survey questions have been formatted into a questionnaire which is designed to help you construct your own survey instrument. You'll have to make changes to use it in your school district or at the school building level.

First, the sample questionnaire is too long to administer. We disregarded any concerns about length to show you a variety of question formats; e.g., closed, open-end, lists, agree-disagree, etc.

Second, this survey instrument is designed to be administered by telephone. That's why it begins with a spoken introduction. You'll also find instructions to interviewers throughout the questionnaire. These instructions are in all caps and boldface type (e.g., **SKIP TO QUESTION 6** or **ASK ONLY OF PARENTS**).

You'll also notice that we "closed" some of the open-end questions. For example, under some questions (e.g., *Where do you get most of your school information?*) we list several possible responses. These responses are not read to respondents. They are included to help interviewers record answers. We know from experience that some people will say they receive school information from newspapers while others will mention school publications. By anticipating these responses we eliminate the need for interviewers to write them every time they're mentioned.

You should also note that whenever an open-end question is closed, there is a category to record answers which weren't anticipated. This category is usually "other," and is followed by a blank line on which interviewers can write the response of the person being interviewed. This is very important.

Of course, if you want to convert this questionnaire to a written survey or if you want to use some of the questions in a focus panel, you'll need to make adjustments. Step-by-step help in available in our workbook titled *The ABC Complete Book of School Surveys*.

Third, this questionnaire is designed for administration to "adult households," including parents and those without school-age children. Again, you'll need to make adjustments if you plan to administer some variation of this questionnaire to parents at Emerson Elementary or to high school students or to business owners in the community.

The Sample Survey

Interviewer's Introduction

Hello, my name is _____, and I'm a volunteer calling for the
_____ Public Schools.

We're conducting a telephone survey to find out what adults in our community think about schools.

You're one of 400 people randomly selected to participate in the survey, and we'd appreciate your help for a few minutes.

Sample Questions

> *Note again that this sample questionnaire cannot be administered as is because of its length and other factors described elsewhere in* The ABC Complete Book of School Marketing.

1. First, how many years have you lived in the _____ School District?

    [1] less than 1 year
    [2] 1-3 years
    [3] 4-6 years
    [4] 7-10 years
    [5] 11 or more years
    [6] no response

2. Do you have school age children?

   [1] yes
   [2] no **(SKIP TO QUESTION 4)**
   [3] no response **(SKIP TO QUESTION 4)**

3. Do they attend public, private, or parochial school?

   [1] public
   [2] private
   [3] parochial
   [4] both public and private/parochial
   [5] home school
   [6] other _____
   [7] no response

4. During the past few years, do you think the quality of public education in our community has gotten better, stayed about the same, or gotten worse?

   [1] better
   [2[same **(SKIP TO PARAGRAPH A)**
   [3] worse **(SKIP TO QUESTION 6)**
   [4] can't say **(SKIP TO PARAGRAPH A)**

5. **IF BETTER**: Why do you feel that way?

   [1] better teachers
   [2] better curriculum
   [3] better principals/administrators
   [4] better school boards
   [5] higher standards
   [6] higher test scores
   [7] other _____
   [8] can't say

6. **IF WORSE:** Why do you feel that way?

   [1] worse teachers
   [2] worse curriculum
   [3] worse principals/administrators
   [4] worse school boards
   [5] lower standards
   [6] lower test scores
   [7] other _____
   [8] can't say

PARAGRAPH A: *During our survey we'll ask you to use a 5-point scale to rate various things. On this scale, 1 is low and 5 is high. Ratings of 2, 3, or 4 are in between.*

7. Let's start by using this 5-point scale to rate the quality of public schools in our state. All things considered, would you give the public schools in our state a rating of 1, 2, 3, 4, or 5?

   [1] 1
   [2] 2
   [3] 3
   [4] 4
   [5] 5
   [6] can't say

8. And what about the public schools here in our community ... would you rate them a 1, 2, 3, 4, or 5?

   [1] 1
   [2] 2
   [3] 3
   [4] 4
   [5] 5
   [6] can't say

9. Some people believe that everyone in the community must work together to create a quality education program. On the 5-point scale, how would you rate our community for the support it provides to the public schools?

   [1] 1
   [2] 2
   [3] 3
   [4] 4
   [5] 5
   [6] can't say

10. People say it's important for students to have a good education. But people think about different things when they think about what makes up a good education. What are some things you think about when you think about a good education?

    [1] quality teachers/staff
    [2] quality instruction in the basics
    [3] diversity of program/services
    [4] high standards
    [5] high test scores
    [6] graduates who go on to college/postsecondary training
    [7] students are prepared for the world of work
    [8] other _____
    [9] can't say

11. What one thing do you think is particularly good about our public schools?

    [1] teachers
    [2] the curriculum/program
    [3] diversity of program/services
    [4] high standards/high test scores
    [5] serve all students
    [6] graduates who go on to college
    [7] students are prepared for the world of work
    [8] other _____
    [9] can't say

12. If you could change one thing in our public schools, what one thing would you change?

[1] return to basics
[2] reduce taxes/cut "fat"/cut funding
[3] accountability
[4] teacher unions/tenure
[5] curriculum component _____
[6] other _____
[7] can't say

Now I'd like to read you a series of statements. After I read each one, please tell me if you strongly agree, somewhat agree, somewhat disagree, or strongly disagree.

	SA	A	D	SD
13. All students should receive instruction in basic core subjects such as reading, mathematics, writing, social studies, and science.	[1]	[2]	[3]	[4]
14. The State should set standards for all students in each of the core subjects.	[1]	[2]	[3]	[4]
15. Regardless of where they live parents should be able to send their child to any public school at public expense.	[1]	[2]	[3]	[4]
16. Regardless of where they live, parents who decide to send their child to private or parochial school should be able to send their child at public expense.	[1]	[2]	[3]	[4]
17. Grades and report cards are good indicators of how well a student is doing in school.	[1]	[2]	[3]	[4]

	SA	A	D	SD
18. All students should serve an apprenticeship or have some kind of work experience before they graduate from high school.	[1]	[2]	[3]	[4]
19. Students who continuously disrupt the learning of others should be removed from regular classrooms and sent to an alternative school at public expense.	[1]	[2]	[3]	[4]
20. Public schools should stop offering nonacademic classes such as driver education.	[1]	[2]	[3]	[4]
21. Schools should turn over the responsibility for competitive team sports like football and basketball to local communities.	[1]	[2]	[3]	[4]
22. Good schools increase the value of your home and other real estate in our community.	[1]	[2]	[3]	[4]
23. Public schools should contract with private companies for things like custodial services, breakfast and lunch programs, and student transportation.	[1]	[2]	[3]	[4]
24. Public schools should contract with private companies for teaching and other instructional services.	[1]	[2]	[3]	[4]
25. Even if it cost taxpayers in your community more money, students should have a longer school day and a longer school year.	[1]	[2]	[3]	[4]

	SA	A	D	SD

26. Student test scores are an important indicator of how well students are doing in school.   [1]   [2]   [3]   [4]

27. Continuing one's education beyond high school is more important today than it was five years ago.   [1]   [2]   [3]   [4]

28. Where do you think young people today are learning the most about manners, morals, and ethics ... from the public schools, the family, the church, or someone else?

    [1] schools
    [2] family
    [3] church
    [4] shared by schools & family
    [5] shared by family & church
    [6] students are not learning manners, morals, and ethics
    [7] other _____
    [8] can't say

Now I'd like to read a list of things public schools could address. Use the 5-point scale to tell me what priority each item should have. Ratings toward 1 indicate a low priority and ratings toward 5 indicate a high priority.

	low				high

29. teaching appreciation of cultural diversity ... would you give that a priority of 1, 2, 3, 4, or 5?   [1]   [2]   [3]   [4]   [5]

30. providing nutrition and health care for poor children   [1]   [2]   [3]   [4]   [5]

31. teaching manners, morals, and ethics   [1]   [2]   [3]   [4]   [5]

32. helping students learn job skills   [1]   [2]   [3]   [4]   [5]

	low				high
33. helping students prepare for college	[1]	[2]	[3]	[4]	[5]
34. helping students learn how to use computers and other technologies	[1]	[2]	[3]	[4]	[5]
35. providing training and professional development courses for teachers and administrators	[1]	[2]	[3]	[4]	[5]
36. helping students cope with problems at home and in their personal lives	[1]	[2]	[3]	[4]	[5]
37. helping parents improve their parenting skills	[1]	[2]	[3]	[4]	[5]

38. People think about different things when they hear the words *local control*. When it comes to education, what do you think about when you hear the words *local control*?

    [1] local school board
    [2] deciding what's best for our children
    [3] determining the school curriculum
    [4] selecting textbooks/learning materials
    [5] deciding how much to spend on education
    [6] making staffing decisions/deciding who to hire
    [7] other _____
    [8] can't say

39. On the 5-point scale, where 1 is not very important and 5 is very important, would you rate the importance of local control a 1, 2, 3, 4, or 5?

    [1] 1
    [2] 2
    [3] 3
    [4] 4
    [5] 5
    [6] can't say

Now I'm going to read you a list of seven things some people believe students should be able to do when they graduate from high school. After I read each one, please tell me who should have primary responsibility for it ... should it be primarily the responsibility of the students, the schools, the family, or should the responsibility be shared by all three.

40. Students should learn to value and be capable of learning over a lifetime ... should this be the responsibility of the student, the schools, the family, or should it be a shared responsibility?

    [1] student
    [2] school
    [3] family
    [4] shared
    [5] can't say

41. Students should learn to be able to apply what they have learned in a variety of situations.

    [1] student
    [2] school
    [3] family
    [4] shared
    [5] can't say

42. Students should learn to be able to make decisions and plans which result in a successful life.

    [1] student
    [2] school
    [3] family
    [4] shared
    [5] can't say

43. Students should learn to become caring, sensitive, and flexible human beings.

   [1] student
   [2] school
   [3] family
   [4] shared
   [5] can't say

44. Students should learn to be creative and innovative.

   [1] student
   [2] school
   [3] family
   [4] shared
   [5] can't say

45. Students should learn to communicate effectively.

   [1] student
   [2] school
   [3] family
   [4] shared
   [5] can't say

46. Students should learn to be competent and productive citizens.

   [1] student
   [2] school
   [3] family
   [4] shared
   [5] can't say

47. Some people say schools should prepare students for the world of work. What kinds of skills do you think students need to be prepared for the world of work?

[1] basic skills
[2] thinking skills (making decisions, solving problems, knowing how to learn)
[3] personal qualities (taking responsibility, self-esteem, sociability, integrity)
[4] knowing how to allocate resources (time, money, materials, staff, space)
[5] interpersonal skills (working on teams, teaching others)
[6] using information
[7] using technology
[8] other _____
[9] can't say

QUESTIONS 48-51 FOR PARENTS OF SCHOOL-AGE CHILDREN ONLY

48. Suppose, at public expense, you could send your child to any school you wanted to -- public, private, or parochial. Would you take your child out of the school he or she now attends?

[1] yes
[2] no **(SKIP TO QUESTION 51)**
[3] can't say **(SKIP TO QUESTION 52)**

49. What's the main reason you would remove your child from the school he or she now attends?

[1] higher quality of instruction
[2] closer to work/family
[3] better discipline
[4] religious training
[5] other _____
[6] can't say

50. Would you send your child to a public, private, or parochial school, or would you teach your child at home? **(GO TO QUESTION 52 AFTER RECORDING RESPONSE)**

   [1] public
   [2] private
   [3] parochial
   [4] home
   [5] can't say

51. **IF NO TO QUESTION 48**: What's the main reason you would leave your child in the school he or she now attends?

   [1] no other educational option available
   [2] transportation problem/excess travel time
   [3] like current school staff
   [4] like current school program/quality of instruction
   [5] other _____
   [6] can't say

52. In your opinion, does our state's school financing system provided more money, less money, or about the same amount of money for the operation of schools than it did last year?

   [1] more
   [2] less
   [3] same
   [4] can't say

53. In the last year, do you think our state's school financing system has helped improve educational quality in our community or not?

   [1] improved quality
   [2] not improved quality
   [3] can't say

Suppose that people in our community were forming a committee to change education. I'm going to read you a list of some people who might be appointed to such a committee. After I read each one, use the 5-point scale to tell me how important it would be to have them on the committee. Ratings toward 1 mean it would not be very important to have them on the committee, and ratings toward 5 mean it would be very important to have them on the committee.

	not very important			very important	
54. local business people ... would you rate the importance of having them on the committee a 1, 2, 3, 4, or 5?	[1]	[2]	[3]	[4]	[5]
55. teachers in our school district	[1]	[2]	[3]	[4]	[5]
56. principals in our school district	[1]	[2]	[3]	[4]	[5]
57. our school administrators	[1]	[2]	[3]	[4]	[5]
58. parents in our community	[1]	[2]	[3]	[4]	[5]
59. local clergy	[1]	[2]	[3]	[4]	[5]
60. students	[1]	[2]	[3]	[4]	[5]
61. local legislators	[1]	[2]	[3]	[4]	[5]
62. local school board members	[1]	[2]	[3]	[4]	[5]
63. college/university professors	[1]	[2]	[3]	[4]	[5]

64. Is there anyone I haven't mentioned that you think should be appointed to a committee to change education?

[1] no
[2] educational experts/consultants
[3] nonparents (people in the community without school-age children)
[4] local government officials
[5] state education officials
[6] other _____
[7] can't say

Now I'm going to read you a list of people and organizations. After I read each one, please use the 5-point scale to tell me how much confidence you have in their ability to improve public education in our state. Ratings toward 1 indicate low confidence, and ratings toward 5 indicate high confidence.

	low confidence			high confidence	
65. local school boards ... would you give them a confidence rating of 1, 2, 3, 4, or 5?	[1]	[2]	[3]	[4]	[5]
66. teachers in your school district	[1]	[2]	[3]	[4]	[5]
67. principals in your school district	[1]	[2]	[3]	[4]	[5]
68. local school administrators	[1]	[2]	[3]	[4]	[5]
69. members of the state legislature	[1]	[2]	[3]	[4]	[5]
70. the governor of our state	[1]	[2]	[3]	[4]	[5]
71. parents in our community	[1]	[2]	[3]	[4]	[5]
72. business people in our community	[1]	[2]	[3]	[4]	[5]
73. teacher unions	[1]	[2]	[3]	[4]	[5]
74. the state board of education	[1]	[2]	[3]	[4]	[5]

75. private companies and educational
    contracts   [1]   [2]   [3]   [4]   [5]

76. When you went to school, did you attend a public, private or parochial
    school?

    [1] public
    [2] private
    [3] parochial
    [4] some combination of 1, 2, and 3
    [5] other _____

77. What's the first thing that comes to mind when you think back to your
    school days?

    [1] a teacher
    [2] a staff member other than a teacher
    [3] the school program/curriculum
    [4] friends
    [5] sports/extracurricular activities
    [6] studying/homework
    [7] other _____
    [8] can't say

78. If you could change something about the school you attended or the
    schooling you received, what would you change?

    [1] teachers
    [2] a curriculum component _____
    [3] rules/regulations
    [4] higher standards
    [5] other _____
    [6] can't say

79. In the past year, have you personally taken any educational classes
    through adult education, a trade school, or a college or university?

    [1] yes
    [2] no

80. Compared to five years ago, how important would you say a college education is to a person's financial well being ... is a college education more important, just as important, or less important today?

[1] more important
[2] just as important
[3] less important
[4] can't say

Finally, we have just a few questions to classify the responses of those participating in the survey.

81. What do you do for a living?

[1] retired
[2] unemployed/laid off
[3] homemaker
[4] other _____

82. In what year were you born?

[1] 1970s
[2] 1960s
[3] 1950s
[4] 1940s
[5] 1930s
[6] 1920 or earlier
[7] declined

83. And finally, what was the last grade in school that you completed?

[1] less than high school
[2] high school graduate
[3] some college
[4] college graduate

That concludes the survey. Thank you very much for your help.

Marketing Tools
Perceptual Profiles

Marketing Tools
Perceptual Profiles

The perception is the reality, and people make decisions on the basis of the "reality" they perceive. But what are some of the forces that shape perceptions?

To provide perspective for this question and help you think about the myriad possibilities, we've prepared a "perceptual profile" of five demographic groups. We start with a group called the *Historicals*, providing a summary list of characteristic behaviors, a few of the things they experienced as they were growing up, a list of some people and events that had significant impact on them, and a couple of "turn offs" and "turn ons." We repeat this profile for each of the subsequent groups.

As we move from one group to another, note that the pace of change quickens -- moving from slow change to rapid change to radical change.

At the conclusion of the profile, we place people on an education-income grid. While any of our five groups can be anywhere on the grid, there is a notable common denominator across the groups: higher levels of education place people at higher levels of income in each of the quadrants.

Obviously, the perceptual profiles are not discrete. Nor are they exhaustive. They are presented here for only one purpose -- to help you think about how people might perceive things and react to change as a result of selected demographic characteristics. You need to ask questions like ...

- Where are the people with these characteristics in my community?

- Are they for us or against us?

- How will they react to our proposals for change?

- Which of their values do I need to address to shape their beliefs?

- What's in my newsletter that appeals to these people?

We hope you find the next several pages stimulating. We know they'll raise questions.

The Historicals

Ages 65 and up, these are the people who capitalized on the opportunities provided by America's unique position in history. The environment they managed was characterized by the end of World War II, pent-up market demands for almost anything that could be produced, and only one country -- America -- with intact production capacity. These are the people who brought the industrial era to its zenith. They made America a superpower economically and militarily. And, they created the baby boom.

characteristic behaviors
- Into organized everything
- Diligent
- Cash-oriented
- Pursue minimal risk risks
- Believe voting is a patriotic duty

what they experienced growing up
- Limited marketplace choices
- A world in which a man's word mattered
- A world in which women stayed home
- A world where you didn't get out of line

people and events influencing their lives
- The Great Depression
- Al Capone
- Hitler
- Roosevelt
- Prohibition

turn offs
- Laziness
- Waste
- Brown-nosing

turn ons
- Radio
- Refrigerators
- Crew cuts
- Friday night dances
- Bath tub gin

The Silver Spoons

Ages 50-65, Silver Spoons were jump-started by the Historicals. Their biggest challenge was accommodating orderly, predictable, linear change and living up to expectations.

characteristic behaviors	• Respect -- sometimes fear -- for authority
	• Materialistic
	• Conservative
	• Goal driven
	• Do things for "the good of the cause"
what they experienced growing up	• Emergence of self-expression
	• Pleasure seeking proliferates
	• Commitments weaken
	• A world where it's fun to get out of line
people and events influencing their lives	• American Bandstand
	• Buddy Holly/Big Bopper/Elvis
	• Ed Sullivan
	• Jonas Salk
	• Penny loafers
	• Sputnik
turn offs	• Girls in slacks
	• Bookworms
	• Going to a dance alone
turn ons	• Drive-in movies
	• Pep bands
	• Phone booth stuffing

The Blurs

Ages 40-50, the Blurs grew up in a period characterized by the rapid pace of linear change. Their history is one of going somewhere fast.

characteristic behaviors	• Anti-establishment/organization
	• Sense of community dissipates
	• Rebellious
	• Skeptical, alienated -- sometimes hostile
	• Short-term goal oriented
	• Question trusted values
what they experienced growing up	• Emergence of dual income family
	• Slowing economic engine
	• Smorgasbord curriculum in schools
	• Science pushes frontiers
people and events influencing their lives	• The Kennedys
	• Martin Luther King
	• Cold War
	• Peace symbol
	• Woodstock
	• Stereo
	• Hair spray
turn offs	• The establishment
	• Authority, especially the military
	• Cleanliness
turn ons	• Mini skirts
	• Muscle cars
	• Rock concerts
	• Leisure suits

Cement Shoe Sequentials

Ages 30-40, the Cement Shoe Sequentials are trying to bring order to life while trudging up hill encumbered by the liabilities of previous generations. As change becomes more radical in its nature, they discover tested methods don't always work and facts are sometimes wrong. They're in the fast lane, but traffic is stop and go.

characteristic behaviors	• Trying to manage change
	• Seeking focus in life
	• Conservative
	• Patriotic
	• Quality conscious
	• Financially extended
what they experienced growing up	• Unconventional households emerge
	• Health consciousness increases
	• Entitlement orientation
	• Science pushes frontiers -- *faster*
people and events influencing their lives	• The Challenger
	• Greenhouse effect/ozone layer depletion
	• AIDS
	• Deregulation
	• Cable/satellite TV
	• Microwaves
	• Personal electronics
turn offs	• The establishment
	• Conformity
turn ons	• Tanning booths
	• Recreational vehicles
	• Professional sports
	• Purposeful clothing

Bobbers

Pre age 25, Bobbers are being buffeted by geometrically accelerating radical change and growing pessimism. Bobbers are often frustrated because the goodies possessed by previous generations seem beyond their grasp.

characteristic behaviors	• Skeptical of authority • Hesitant risk-takers • Seeking stability • Financially at-risk • Short-term goal oriented
what they experienced growing up	• Meaningful work options decline • Television creates unreal perspectives • Leaders and heroes disappear
people and events influencing their lives	• Chernobyl • Collapse of communism • Cold War ends • Countries dissolve and reconfigure • Ethnic tensions • The Gulf War
turn offs	• Bureaucracy • Old ways of doing things • Politicians
turn ons	• Professional sports • Lifestyle recreation • Being casual • Talk television/radio

Now we can create a four-quadrant grid, using education and income to position people by what they believe and value. Here's the grid:

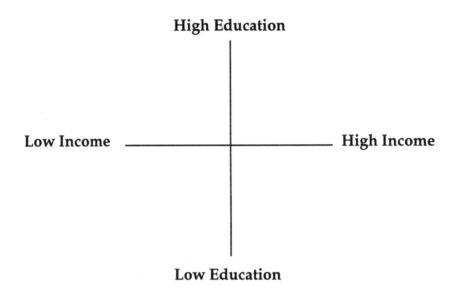

Next, we can assign names to each of the quadrants. This will make them easier to describe, and more intriguing to assess. Let's call the upper left the Coffee Fringe, the upper right the Power Pack, the lower left the Empties, and the lower right the Cheap Wines, as follows:

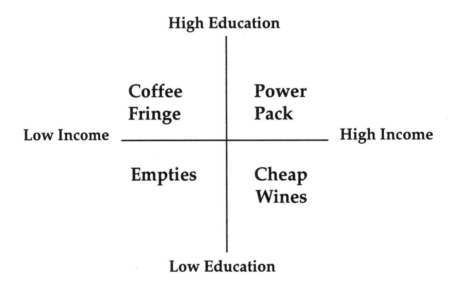

Here's a description of people in each of the quadrants. As you read the questions, repeat the questions asked at the beginning of this section -- e.g., What's in my newsletter that will appear to this group?

The Coffee Fringe (High education/Low income)

Descriptors

- Liberal
- Scheming
- Skeptical
- Indecisive
- Unfulfilled

Favorite TV program	• Nightline
Favorite food	• Low-fat anything
Favorite drink	• Coffee
Primary mode of travel	• On foot
Dream destination	• Europe
Most recent purchase	• Jeans
Big night on the town	• Bookstore browsing

The Power Pack (High education/High income)

Descriptors

- Self-confident
- Politically conservative
- Self-confident
- Financially stable
- Stubborn

Favorite TV program	• Meet the Press
Favorite food	• Caesar salad
Favorite drink	• Bottled water
Primary mode of travel	• Foreign luxury car
Dream destination	• A private island
Most recent purchase	• From a catalog
Big night on the town	• A movie or play and dessert

Empties (Low education/Low income)

Descriptors

- Narrow perspective
- Frustrated
- Heavy TV watchers
- Aimless
- Want expedient change
- View the world as a terrifying place

Favorite TV program	• Talk anything
Favorite food	• Burgers
Favorite drink	• Domestic beer
Primary mode of travel	• Previously owned vehicle
Dream destination	• Mall of the Americas
Most recent purchase	• Lottery ticket
Big night on the town	• Bowling

Cheap Wines (Low education/High income)

Descriptors

- Self-centered
- Wanna-bes
- Champion micro-causes
- Live in the past

Favorite TV program	• Any shopping channel
Favorite food	• Pasta
Favorite drink	• Mixed drinks
Primary mode of travel	• Domestic luxury car
Dream destination	• Las Vegas
Most recent purchase	• A tabloid
Big night on the town	• Buttered popcorn and romance movies

Marketing Tools
Guidelines for facilitating

Marketing Tools
Guidelines for facilitating

Creating change requires that you facilitate -- not direct -- change.

As a facilitator you'll have to play a variety of roles to successfully implement The MDS process.

Being a facilitator is challenging because it requires a complex combination of skills -- leading and following, listening and talking, questioning and summarizing. At times, you'll have to seize the initiative and present your own description of environmental change. At other times, you'll have to act as a sponge, absorbing information without reacting to it.

- *If facilitating is not one of your competencies, seek help.* Recruit a staff member, a colleague, or an outsider to work for you. (Then make sure that you are 110% attentive to the process.)

- *Facilitators must be flexible.* You must be able to amend The MDS process so that it fits your needs. If you can't hold the meetings according to the format that we've outlined, then you'll have to change the format to fit your circumstances.

  If you need more time to complete a given task, take it. If you want to go through the entire process in a weekend retreat, then organize to do that.

- *Give everyone involved a chance to participate.* No one should feel like the process is being used to force-feed an existing agenda. For instance, someone with desktop publishing skills could make the material in the Appendixes into an outstanding plan -- it would look great and be well written -- but it wouldn't have the commitment that comes from ownership. That's what you're facilitating -- ownership and commitment.

In addition to your facilitating skills, consider three other things:

The facility   Make sure that the facility you use for planning is conducive to the process. Use tables and comfortable chairs. Have refreshments available. Understand the attitude-enhancing benefits of things that set your planning meeting apart from others: things like fresh fruit, mints, cold soft drinks, and other pleasantries.

Well before your participants arrive, check to see that the room is properly equipped and that the equipment works. Great content can be devastated by poor projection equipment, hot rooms, and crackling microphones.

The people you select   If you involve representatives of your staff and community, make sure that you invite people "who don't have time to be there." Seek out the high-speed, high-credibility people. They seem to have a monopoly on ideas and energy, and they'll make it easier to explain the process and its products to the rest of the staff and community when you're finished.

How you process the participants   When you do small group work (such as identifying change priorities), limit the group's size to a half-dozen people. Anything bigger is a mob ... and mobs do dangerous things!

Marketing Tools
Keys to effective publications

Marketing Tools
Keys to effective publications

If you weren't you, would you read your publications?

People read less today. In fact, some say we live in a soundbite world that has a bumper sticker mentality. While that may be extreme, people do scan more, skipping through things they read.

What is this new breed of scanners seeking? Something of interest to them. Sometimes they know what it is. Other times they don't.

This brief analysis tells you that you have to write something of interest and provide it to those who are interested. Or, you have to do something to create an interest so that people will read what you have written.

Remember that people are increasingly visual in their orientation. But even visuals have to have impact . (The class picture doesn't have impact. Anytime someone's head is pin-sized, there isn't any impact. When people have to squint, there isn't any impact. When a picture is out of focus, there isn't any impact. The photos in *National Geographic* have impact.)

Before people can read your publication they have to pick it up. That's why the appearance of your publication is extremely important. Try this test: put ten or twenty publications -- including yours -- on a table. Ask a few people to pick up the publications that look interesting. Then ask why they picked the publications they did.

When people look at your publications, they're looking at you. Your publications -- just like you -- are ambassadors for your organization. If you weren't you, would you read them? Believe them? Be moved by them?

■ Write headlines that tell a story. Some people only read headlines. Make sure your headline readers learn something.

- Ask yourself what your publication is attempting to communicate. But communicating a story or idea is only a part of the job. Help your readers interpret. Don't assume that people will make inferences, see relationships, or draw conclusions.

- Make your publications attractive. Remember, when people look at your publication, they're looking at you.

- Create a layout that is easy to read. Filling the paper with type makes a publication uninviting and difficult to read. Don't be afraid of leaving "white space."

- Include the name, address and telephone number of the building or school district. Let your readers know whom to contact for more information.

- Read your last newsletter cover to cover. After each article ask, "How many people really care about this?" Don't write about that topic again if your honest assessment is "not many people are interested."

- A good rule of thumb: never include more than three people in a photo. Two is better. One is best. And a close-up of the one provides *impact*. Use photos that are crisp and clear. Crop unnecessary distractions in the background to help focus your reader's attention.

- Ask yourself what story your photo tells ... or what emotion it stirs. If photos are used to accompany an article, make sure they give the reader greater insight into the topic.

- Make sure your readers can tell where your publication is from and what it's about ... at a glance.

- Use quality printing to enhance the overall look of your publication.

- Use up-to-date clip art to improve the look of your publication. Too much clip art is amateurish and can deter a reader's attention.

- Write captions for all photos. Tell your reader who is doing what and why they are doing it.
- Set all type in upper and lower case. Use **boldface** to highlight key points. Type that is set in all capital letters is hard to read, and there's some evidence that it *de-emphasizes* the message.

- Use charts and graphs to help your readers understand a situation or idea. Make sure they enhance the information you've shared in the article.

- Use words and descriptions that your audience will understand. Don't bog down your newsletter with educational jargon.

- Use lead sentences that are strong enough to capture the attention of readers.

- Have an "outsider" read your publication for content, design, and overall appeal prior to printing.

- Use a writing style that is appropriate to your target audience. (Most newspapers are written at the ninth or tenth grade reading level. Unfortunately, most school publications are written at the 16th grade level or above!)

- Assess the job you are doing. Ask yourself ...

  - What do I like best about this publication?
  - What could be improved?
  - What other information should be included?
  - If I weren't me, would I read this?

Wier on publications

Ken Wier is a school-community relations administrator in Pennsylvania. For the past twenty years Ken has produced some of the best school publications in America. He also judges publication contests and critiques publications for the National School Public Relations Association. The following are some of his thoughts on effective school publications.

School publications that produce results are targeted. They provide information someone (the target) needs or wants. Those that receive awards address the concerns of their readers.

Sometimes writers forget that the newsletter or special topic brochure will be influential only if it connects with the recipient and helps focus him/her on the topics presented.

Successful writers know that their readers are busy people. They know that they must compete for their readers' time and attention. They know that they must be concise, direct, and tuned into the concerns of readers.

Where do you begin if you want to create the near-perfect school publication? Clearly the best place to start is with a need, a good idea, and a commitment to publish something attractive, useful, and informative.

Work smart -- Be prepared all the time

Good ideas often come at inconvenient times. Be ready to capture your best ideas. Some of our best thoughts come to us while we drive, or shower -- while we jog or work outside.

Veteran writers and editors know that these ideas shouldn't be lost. They stop and find a notepad. These are the people you see talking into a recorder at the traffic light.

Set aside time to think about your publications. While that may seem obvious, when is the last time you did it? Producing a publication without a rough sketch, a theme, a mock-up, or an outline is a big mistake.

Always keep your goals in mind

Some school administrators produce publications to win awards in local, state, or national contests. While this may bring positive recognition to your school district, it shouldn't be the primary motivation for producing a publication. Acceptance by consumers should be the goal of every writer, editor, designer, and publisher.

The best publications get results. They influence thinking. They entice readers to consider options and encourage them to learn more about the subject. They provide readers with quotable quotes and facts that can be remembered.

School publications are rarely created to entertain; most often they are designed to inform, to influence, or to sell an idea.

Keep budget in mind

Knowing what the finished publication will cost is essential. Your budget may need to cover costs for the photographer, writer, designer, typographer, and printer. Many projects can't be completed without the related costs of envelopes, postage, and mailing services. Understanding the total cost of the project is important.

Sharpen your focus

The best publications focus on people. This has been confirmed by advertising research, and is evident in the best magazines and the best newspapers. People like to read about other people. They like to look at photos of happy people, thoughtful people, and -- sometimes -- sad or unfortunate people.

Schools are the ideal location for wonderful photo opportunities. Students are among the most photogenic subjects in the world. Photographs of students can provide an image that will be remembered long after the written words are forgotten.

School publications need a clear purpose and a strong voice. The purpose should be apparent and the voice should be that of the agency or the institution. Articles should not be written in the first person unless they are signed pieces that clearly represent the opinions or experiences of the author. Most publications that are produced on a planned schedule have a well-established voice and tone.

Know the principles of good design

Publications that attract attention have a crisp and appropriate design. The design directs readers' attention and keeps them moving through the publication. Good design is comfortable. Good design is appropriate to the message and the feeling that is being communicated.

Judges of publication contests often describe the winning pieces as those that have an *appealing* quality. The winning publications are appealing because designers have given attention to detail and spent time and effort producing clear headlines, pullout quotes, and photo captions.

Understanding that some readers will do little more than read the headlines, the pullout quotes, and the photo captions provides a reminder that these items must be powerful if they are to attract attention and hold the readers' interest.

Pay attention to your writing

Well-written copy is essential. The text should be thoughtfully prepared and carefully edited. It should be read by several people who bring different viewpoints to the proofreading assignment. Some of these readers can look for faulty construction or unclear meaning; others can read for content problems.

Someone should look at the technical side of the content. In other words, will the classroom teacher, the bus driver, or the custodian be comfortable with the manner in which the information is presented? It's damaging to have an informed reader get the feeling that the writer didn't really understand the subject.

Give the eyes a place to rest

All too frequently, school publications are overcrowded with type and "stuffed" with small photographs and clip art around featured copy. The overcrowded page doesn't provide a place for the eyes to rest. White space (or blank space) provides relief from too much to see, too much to read, and too much to think about. Quality design provides room for readers to breathe -- room for readers to stop and think about the material being presented. That's why effective use of white space is critical to the overall success of the publication.

Select your photographs wisely

The best photographs can have more impact on readers than pages of copy. Photos should be large and selected to evoke a reaction. Some should make you smile. Others should cause you to remember your student days or childhood. And some photos should shout, "Look at me! I'm learning and I like it." Others should leave readers with the impression that teachers are doing a good job.

Avoid photos that feature awards being distributed or the prearranged hand-shake. Lineup photos are awful. Most photos shouldn't have more than five or six people in them. Large groups rarely create any photographic message beyond the obvious: *look at this large group.*

Always order more copies than you you think need. The additional copies are inexpensive and may be needed in the future. Reorders are expensive.

Tips for building-level newsletters

In a typical school community the most popular (and most trusted) school publication is the building-level newsletter. This publication is usually created by the school secretary, the building principal, a parent editor, or a combination of people.

Here's how to make your newsletter more interesting, more attractive, and more valuable:

- *The ideal low-budget newsletter consists of four pages* that are 8 1/2 x 11 inches. Quality copies can be produced by a quick copy shop or on school copy machines. Mimeograph and ditto machines cannot produce the quality you want.

- *Building-level newsletters are often filled with "clip art."* Most critics of these newsletters believe that a little clip art goes a long way. Too many designs and too much canned art detracts from the overall attractiveness of the newsletter.

- *Original drawings should be used with great care.* Student art should be used sparingly.

- *Photographs should be used only when the newsletter will be printed on production equipment.* Photographs should be high quality and displayed for maximum benefit. They should be cropped to feature people and to eliminate distracting backgrounds. Photographs of children at work and those featuring interaction between a teacher and a child are the best. Small photographs aren't acceptable. Most judges of school publication contests dislike the photo montage. They consider it a gimmick or a space-filler.

■ *Ink color should always be black* -- or appear to be black. A deep charcoal gray or a deep navy blue can be effective on the right paper. But selection of these inks would only apply to those newsletters being printed professionally.

Photos should never be printed in color ink. Faces never look good when printed in green ink -- or blue, red, or purple.

■ *Color inks should not be used for typed copy in holiday issues.* An entire newsletter printed in green ink to observe St. Patrick's Day is a sure way to ruin the March issue.

Readers have difficulty with any typed copy printed in color. However, headline type in color is acceptable when used in moderation.

■ *Typed material should never be superimposed over art or photographic images.* For example, you should never publish a story over a drawing of the school seal or school mascot.

■ *Building-level newsletters are the perfect place for regular features.* "The Parent's Corner," "Notes from the Librarian," or a feature from the cafeteria manager soon become expected features that attract regular readership.

Readers like to get comfortable with their favorite publications and usually begin by looking for the section or feature that they enjoy most. A simple clip art design that identifies this regular feature helps to establish recognition and develop reader loyalty.

■ *The individual school newsletters should be friendly, easy to read, and filled with news and ideas that readers will find useful.* Everyone writing for the newsletter should avoid formal, stiff sentence construction. The best rule is to write the way you talk. The newsletter is not the place for jargon or educational acronyms.

■ *The building-level newsletter should be short, simple, direct, informational, educational, and easily understood.*

Marketing Tools
Developing a promotional campaign

Developing a local promotional campaign

Public Service Advertising (PSA) has proved to be an effective way for public agencies to get their messages out. You can use a PSA program to reach large numbers efficiently. It is an excellent vehicle for providing information and influencing understanding and behavior.

But many obstacles often prevent groups from making the most of these marketing efforts. Among them:

- *Tough competition for space and time.* Media willing to use space for PSA programs often have more people requesting help than they have space to offer.

- *Poor creative and technical quality.* Many organizations lack the expertise to produce top-quality programming that is up to media standards.

- *Lack of the frequency needed to ensure results.* Since many PSA programs get space that media are unable to otherwise sell or use, their messages suffer from the lack of repeated exposure that's needed to make them work.

Improving your odds

To help even the odds in getting a good media response to your efforts you should:

- create advertisements that meet the technical quality your media want;
- develop a message that is appealing and presented well; and,
- use only the format that meets what your media need (ad size for print, length for broadcast, and so on).

Although it's not necessary, it often helps to localize your messages as much as possible. Obviously, media considering your PSA program will be more likely to help if the messages relate directly to people in the geographic area that they serve. You can accomplish this by always including the name of your district or even individual schools. A tagline that includes a local phone number where people can seek out more information may help as well.

Getting started

The first step, overlooked all too often, is contacting the media that you'd like to work with as early as possible. It's usually a good idea to make this initial contact through someone in your organization or community who has some type of relationship with the media executive you're contacting.

One good place to look for a liaison is with major commercial advertisers in your district that you know. You may have a board member or parent volunteer whose business is a significant local advertiser. That person can help make the initial contact. And, as an advertiser, your liaison will make sure that your initial request for information gets the attention it needs.

Although a media organization's advertising director is a logical place to start, consider contacting a newspaper's publisher or broadcaster's general manager in the "information-seeking round."

At first you're not looking for a hard commitment. You're seeking a get-acquainted meeting to review your ideas. Get some feedback on how your ideas match that medium's commitment to offering public-service time and space.

At this initial meeting you'll get a better understanding of the types of programs that area media are willing to sponsor and how soon they may be able to accommodate a program such as yours.

You can also get a look at the types of PSA materials that the medium may be using now. This might give you some ideas to help you move the design of your materials forward.

Don't get discouraged

It's not uncommon to hear all kinds of reasons why the media may not be able to help -- and it's not uncommon to get only tentative offers of support.

With only lukewarm expressions of support and a tight budget for making this work, you might ask why you should consider going forward at all. But don't get discouraged too fast. There are several more things you should consider to increase your chances of succeeding:

■ *Look outside for help in getting ad space and time.* Many businesses in your community -- large and small -- may be interested in helping secure ad space by underwriting the cost of your ad placements.

If they already advertise, they'll be in a good position to secure the space at an excellent cost, and they'll benefit when they are portrayed locally as an organization that's willing to support important community efforts such as yours.

■ *You may be able to develop support from a group of sponsors, so no one business is asked to shoulder the cost.*

Get your program together, define just what you want, and then start contacting local business groups or businesses through contacts, such as employees, board members, parents, and others.

A big bonus in going this way: You won't suffer the sporadic schedule that often accompanies PSA programs using only donated space and time.

■ *Look inside and outside for creative and production help.* You may need a lot of help to identify the individuals who will be featured in your ads. You may also need help in creating your messages and copy. And you may need help in producing camera-ready art and broadcast quality audio and video.

■ *Of course, you can look to your own staff for help in all three areas, but don't overlook the many ways in which outsiders can get involved and make your program better.*

If you have one media outlet that's a willing partner, it may be able to lend a hand in the creative and production tasks. But don't count on too much media help. Their internal resources often are thin -- and frequently overloaded. And, of course, they are already playing a role in helping you to get the space or air time you want.

Businesses in the community may be better equipped to help in these tasks. Area advertising or marketing agencies can sometimes be encouraged to take on such *pro bono* tasks. And area colleges often have programs offering student help.

Don't let a lack of knowledge or scarce resources keep your programming from happening. There probably are many people in the community who have the expertise and will be happy to share it with you.

■ *Look beyond traditional media for space and time.* Local newspapers, radio and TV stations, and cable outlets are usually first on the PSA program wish list.

But other outlets can reach your targets just as well. Seek out ways in which you may be able to use transit ads, weekly and neighborhood publications, school and community newsletters and publications, student media, and posters in public buildings, retail shops, and businesses.

Get creative when you consider alternative uses for your materials. For example, if you produce a TV spot, ask local video-rental shops to include it with your audio PSA spots with other broadcasts going out over the public address systems. Or ask local retailers to include your print ads with billings or other customer mailings.

Putting your ideas into action

The following pages offer you some guidance on what PSA spots in your program could look and sound like.

Many of the examples here rely on resources that you already have — successful people in your community who are products of your schools. They are living examples of the promise and power offered in a public school education and they are living examples of what today's schools are doing for today's children. They can power your messages and offer instant credibility.

Using celebrity spokespersons has been a well-used PSA technique for years. While the models shown here could be used with celebrity spokespersons, they don't depend on it. The messages here are tailored to work with people found in almost every community. You'll find an assortment of messages, slogans, formats, and techniques. Study them all. Feel free to adapt what you see here -- or borrow it outright -- for your own program.

Broadcast

Television, radio and cable

Teacher/Student

Anncr: ABC third-grade teacher Margaret Smith is about
to confront Attorney Joe Jones. Let's listen in:

(traffic sounds)

Smith: Joseph, you remember the trouble you had with
spelling. In fact you told me you hated it. Now
you're a big-time lawyer using words every day
in search of justice. Just what do you have
to say for yourself?

Jones: Thanks, Miss Smith. And thank you ABC Public
Schools.

Anncr: ABC Public Schools. We're building futures one a
a time.

Administrator/Student

Anncr: ABC High Principal Mary Black is giving
police chief Tom Brown some trouble. Let's
listen in:

(traffic sounds)

Smith: Back in high school you told me math was a waste
of time. Now you're a police chief who had
no trouble figuring out how fast I was driving
just now. What do you have to say for yourself,
Chief Brown?

Jones: Thanks, Mrs. Black. And thank you ABC Public
Schools.

Anncr: ABC Public Schools. We're building futures
one at a time.

Former Student

Anncr: John Jones is a successful CPA right here in ABC.
He's finally going to reveal his secret of
success. Let's listen in:

Jones: Ask me how I got ahead and I'll give you the same
old answers. Hard work. Dedication. Going the
extra mile. But guess what? That's all true.
But the question to really ask is how I got
started. And to answer that, I have to say,
"Thank you ABC Public Schools."

Anncr: ABC Public Schools. We're building futures one
at a time.

Administrator/Student

Anncr: ABC Superintendent Lester Quick is taking on the
local media again. Let's listen in.

Quick: So, Mary Morton, you're an important reporter at
the ABC Press. Back in your school days you were
pretty good at telling stories -- especially when

you were late for class. What do you have to say
for yourself, Ms. Morton?

Morton: Thanks, Doctor Quick. And thank you ABC Public
Schools.

Anncr: ABC Public Schools. Look at what we've done.
Look at what we're doing.

Parent

Anncr: Ken Osburn owns the McDonald's restaurant right
here in ABC. He thinks he's a successful busi-
nessman. But his mother's about to give us the
real story. Let's listen in:

Osburn: When Kenny was in grade school he used to whine
about work all the time. Some days I wondered what would happen to that boy. I'm not
sure just how it happened. But I do have a say,
thanks, ABC Public Schools.

Anncr: ABC Public Schools. We're always starting some
thing great.

Student

Anncr: Newscaster Jamie Smith is covering a breaking
story. Let's go to her live now. Jamie, what
can you tell us?

Smith: This is Jamie Smith with an important development
(pause). I wrote this (pause). And I read this
(pause). Not bad for a local kid, wouldn't you

say? Oh, and one more thing, thanks, ABC Public Schools.

Anncr: ABC Public Schools. We get people started right.

Video   **Student (video version)**

Anchor at desk   Anncr: Newscaster Jamie Smith dis-
                          covering a breaking story.
                          Let's go to her live now.
                          Jamie, what can you tell us?

Reporter
on street   Smith: This is Jamie Smith with an
                          important development. (pause)
                          I wrote this. (pause) And I can
                          read this. (pause) Not bad for
                          a local kid, (Fade) wouldn't you
                          say? Oh, and one more thing,
                          thanks ABC Public Schools.

V/O logo   Anncr: ABC Public Schools. We get
Slogan   people started right.

Fade

Teacher

Anncr: If you're thinking about quitting school --
          or if you know someone who is -- you'd
          better hear what Mary Smith has to say.

Smith: Back in the good old days, before you were
          even born, I started teaching in the ABC
          Public Schools. But you know what? I can
          still remember some things about former
          students that they've probably forgotten.

284

Let's see ... there's Joe Flannery. Used to be
a flashy dresser. He manages service at the
Ford dealership now. Mary Smith always
loved gym class. She was elected Mayor over
in Bridgetown. Kate Mellon's a lawyer. Bill
Smith is a successful insurance adjuster.
Joe Jones runs the Family Cafe. May Quick's
a doctor now. Leon Henry? President of
Quick Frozen Foods. Jim Brown? News director at WABC. Jack Staples? ... (voice
trails).

Anncr: ABC Public Schools. Stay in and win.

Video   Teacher (video version)

V/O school front   Anncr: If you're thinking about
at dismissal   quitting school -- or if you
                              know someone who is -- you'd
                              better hear what Mary Smith
                              Smith has to say.

at desk   Smith: Back in the good old days,
                              before you were even born, I
                              started teaching at ABC
                              Public Schools. But you
                              know what? I can still
                              remember some things
Blurs to "memory"   about former students that
                              they've probably forgotten.
                              Let's see ... there's Joe
Faces of students   Flannery. Used to be a
                              flashy dresser. He manages
                              a service at the Ford
                              dealership now.

	Mary Smith always loved gym class. She was elected Mayor over in Bridgetown.
Back to Smith at desk	Kate Mellon's a lawyer. Bill Smith is a successful insurance adjuster. Joe Jones runs the Family Cafe. Mary Quick's a doctor now. Leon Henry? President of Quick Frozen Foods. Jim Brown?
News director at WABC V/O logo Fade.	Jack Staples? ... (voice trails).
	Anncr: ABC Public Schools. Stay in and win.

Businessman

Anncr: A lot of people looking for jobs find one with Jake Johnson at Worldwide Industries. In fact Jake hired more than 50 people last year alone. Tell us Jake, what does it take to get a job with your company?

Johnson: There really isn't much in common about the people I've hired. Some are young. Some aren't young. Some are short. Some are tall. Some are men. Some are women. Oh year, there is one thing in common. They all graduated from school.

Anncr: Your diploma. Don't leave school without it. ABC Public Schools.

```
Video            Businessman (video version)

Reporter on street   Anncr:  A lot of people looking for
facing camera shot           jobs find one with Jake
widens to include            Johnson at Worldwide Indus-
Johnson.  Reporter           tries.  In fact, Jake hired
turns to Johnson             more than 50 people last
                             year alone.  Tell us Jake,
                             what does it take to get a
                             job with your company?


Johnson into     Johnson:  There really isn't much in
camera                     common about the people I've
                           hired. Some are young.  Some
Return to 2 shot           aren't young. Some are tall.
Reporter turns to          Some are short.  Some are
camera                     men.  Some are women.  Oh
                           yea, there is one thing in
                           common.  They all graduated
                           from school.


Reporter into
Camera           Anchr:    Your diploma.  Don't leave
                           school without it.  ABC
Super BPS                  Public Schools.

Fade
```

It's finally all adding up

"Thanks, ABC Public Schools."

Joe Jones, CPA
Managing Partner, Jones & Jones
Graduate, ABC Public Schools

ABC Public Schools

Where futures are built

The sky is my limit

"Thanks, ABC Public Schools."

James Conklin
Major, U.S. Air Force
Graduate, ABC Public Schools

ABC Public Schools

Where futures are built

It's good medicine

"Thanks, ABC Public Schools."

Carl Anderson, RN
Head Nurse, Memorial Hospital
Graduate, ABC Public Schools

ABC Public Schools

Where futures are built

I'm still doing homework

"Thanks, ABC Public Schools."

Sara Smyth-Barton
ABC Century 21
Graduate, ABC Public Schools

ABC Public Schools

Where futures are built

Marketing Tools
It's everybody's responsibility

Marketing Tools
It's everybody's responsibility

One person cannot *do* marketing for an entire system. Nor is marketing something a team or task force can *do*.

Individuals can orchestrate and support marketing, but you can't assign marketing to one person and expect that person to market everyone and everything in the system.

Task forces and teams can't assume that responsibility either. They can facilitate, nurture and guide, but they can't *do* marketing.

Marketing is one of those things that's everyone's responsibility. Just as every person in an organization should have a degree of competence, everyone should be a part of the marketing process.

Think about it: we don't assign organizational competence to a person or team. We don't say, "You're responsible for the competence of the system."

Individuals can orchestrate programming which helps people increase their competence, and teams can facilitate and nurture and guide the pursuit of competence. But, in the end, being competent is everyone's individual responsibility. The same is true in the case of marketing.

We've already said that marketing is a process. We believe that marketing begins at the policy level. You'll find some thoughts on the school board's role in marketing elsewhere in *Appendix B*. (See *Marketing Tools: Characteristics of effective school boards.*)

We've also said that marketing is something everyone needs to take personally. (Refer back to *Marketing in action: Take it personally.*)

So what are some of the communication and public relations things individuals in a school system can do to support the marketing initiative? On the following pages you'll find a host of ideas and techniques. These ideas and techniques -- adapted from the tip sheets in Banach, Banach & Cassidy's *Champions for Children*® program -- speak to things bus drivers, custodians, principals, secretaries, and teachers can *do*.

Things bus drivers can do

There's no doubt that school bus drivers have a challenging job. They have to rise early, cope with changing traffic and weather conditions, exhibit the highest safety standards, get youngsters to school on time, *and* help set the tone for the day.

Getting kids to school safely and on time is what everyone expects school bus drivers to do. Helping them arrive ready to learn is another matter. Not many people would list "preparing students for learning" as part of a bus driver's job, yet it may be one of the most important contributions that bus drivers make.

For many students, the bus driver represents the beginning and end of the school day. A simple greeting, a name-mention, a caring question, a smile -- all are low effort-high impact ways bus drivers can help youngsters get the day off to a good start. They are also techniques that can help students turn the corner on a rough morning. While on the way home, the same caring attitude puts a positive cap on the school day.

Educators salute bus drivers who "smile them on and cheer them off." These drivers help shape what goes into the classroom in the morning, and the attitude that goes home in the evening. They are important ambassadors who smooth the road to learning.

Tips on technique

- Be polite. Give students a *please* and *thank you*, and you'll get the same politeness back.

- Get involved in holiday and school themes. It can make the ride to and from school extra special.

- Be cheerful. Greet students with a smile and a good morning greeting. Little things set a positive tone for the day (and being positive is more fun than being a grump!).

- Be attentive. Noticing a new haircut or article of clothing can really brighten a youngster's day. (Think about how you feel when someone says something nice about you.)

- Answer questions from parents promptly. Every question parents ask is important to them, and -- in their eyes -- their child is the *only* child riding your bus.

- Be sensitive to the feelings of young riders. For many of them riding a bus is their first school adventure without Mom, Dad, or some other adult.

- Make sure young children have a place to go when they get off the bus. Ask them if they know where to go if no one is home.

- Get to know the staff and administration of every school you serve. When discipline problems occur, make sure administrators are aware of them. Tell them you'd also appreciate knowing more about the children who ride with you. If there's a child with a problem or medical condition, you ought to be aware of that up front.

- Sometimes bus drivers are the only school person with whom parents have daily contact. To them, *you* are the school. Make sure your positive, caring attitude is showing. What people think of you is often what they think of the entire school district.

- Reward good behavior. Positive reinforcement is the best way to nurture the positive actions of others.

- Figure out how you can alert parents and riders when there are going to be unavoidable delays.

- Let riders know how you expect them to behave. Tell them you can't tolerate behaviors which could risk the safety of passengers.

- Talk with students who are consistently running to the bus stop because they're late. Challenge them to be on time.

- Pay attention to unfamiliar faces at bus stops. If they are strangers to your riders, something strange may be in the works. Alert your supervisor or local law enforcement officials.

- Allow a few minutes at the start of the school year to answer parents' questions and to accommodate the first-day pictures.

Things custodians can do

La Caminata is Spanish for "the walk." In South America the words are often used to describe a tour of the neighborhood by two of the most important people in the school -- the principal (the person who runs the school) and the custodian (the person who takes care of the school).

The idea is a good one. It allows two people with extremely high credibility to tell the school story. It works in North America, too.

To be sure, the job of the school custodian has become more varied and complex. Today, "keeping the boiler fired" has gone the way of the steam locomotive. Custodians now need to understand a host of things, including safety codes, federal regulations, basic maintenance, and the chemistry of waxes. They also have to function as public relations agents for the schools.

One of the most visible parts of the custodian's job is keeping the school "dressed for success." The first impressions people have about a school are usually determined by how the school looks. In fact, the school's exterior often becomes the basis for long-term perceptions of what is happening on its interior. For many people, a well maintained building symbolizes quality people operating a quality educational program.

While caring for the school and providing a safe and secure learning environment are important responsibilities, they're only a part of the job. The custodian also helps make the educational program work. By caring for the classrooms and the people in them, custodians enhance the staff's capacity to provide quality educational programming.

Every successful school has an effective custodian. And, while you can't see everything a good custodian does, it's easy to spot the schools that don't have one.

<u>Tips on technique</u>

- Set high standards. By keeping your building in good condition, your school can become a source of pride to students. In return, they're more likely to treat their learning facility with more respect.

■ Let staff and students know what it takes to keep their school in A-1 shape. Sometimes knowing leads to helping.

■ Be safety conscious. Your attentiveness can prevent accidents and injuries.

■ Reward good behavior with a kind word and a smile. It's one of the things people remember about custodians long after they've graduated.

■ Anticipate. Being on top of things helps make things run smoothly, and it reflects well on everybody in the school.

■ Alert staff and students when you have a project that might impact them. Letting them know about an inconvenience can make things more convenient for everyone.

■ Custodians have high credibility in the community. People believe what they say. So, be a good ambassador for your school. Know what's going on and be there when it's time to squelch a rumor.

■ Be a role model for students. They notice what you say and do, so say and do things you'd like them to say and do.

Things principals can do

Principals are key influentials who work at the front lines of the educational enterprise. They are among the first to know when things are going well, and they're often the first to hit the potholes.

Effective schools research speaks to the importance of good principals. In fact, it has become accepted convention that you can't have a good school without a good principal.

Effective principals know how to bring people together and mobilize resources for initiatives which are in the best interest of young people. And there can be little doubt that the effectiveness of school-community relations is usually dependent on the tone set by principals.

Tips on technique

- Mail notes home which commend children, even when their accomplishments aren't monumental.

- Remind teachers to end the school day by telling students what they learned during the day.

- Encourage staff members to alert you to activities which have news potential.

- Have some way of recognizing the regular kid -- the one who isn't an academic whiz or an athletic all-star. (These kids make up most of your student body!)

- Regularly monitor what people in your attendance area saying about schools.

- Host mini-tours for senior citizens, real estate agents, parents, district bus drivers, and others.

- Showcase student accomplishments at service clubs ... in malls ... downtown ... at airports ... anywhere!

- Help staff members define meaningful parent involvement. Communicate this to parents on a classroom-by-classroom basis.

- Send cards ... to staff members and school VIPs on their birthdays ... to students when they have an extended illness ... to say thank you.

- Have a buddy system to help newcomers -- staff, students, and parents -- feel welcome and at ease in your school.

- Have a bulletin board where you can display newspaper articles and other items of interest about your staff and students. Boost readership by posting a joke of the week. Or invite people to write captions for a cartoon. (Have staff and student categories. Then appoint a committee to name a weekly winner in each category.)

- Have a "wall of fame" where you can post information about school alumni and parents of current students.

- Provide staff members with training in customer relations and effective communication.

- Help people see the big picture. Create forums where you can have discussions on the forces of change.

- Stress the importance of treating every school visitor in a friendly and courteous manner.

- Send notes of commendation to the homes of staff members. Consider mailing a thank you note to an employee's spouse and children. Thank them for sharing him/her with your students and colleagues. Impact!

- Get your entire staff -- bus drivers, cafeteria staff, custodians, teachers -- together regularly to talk about "what's up" and to dialogue on problems and opportunities.

- Model life-long learning. Let students and staff catch you reading, thinking, or browsing on the computer.

Things school secretaries can do

When people want school information, they say they call "the school." What they really mean is that they call the school secretary because to many people the secretary is "the school."

School secretaries are among the most credible school employees. Their high regard is easy to understand. The school secretary generally lives in the community and has daily contact with students, teachers, and members of key external audiences such as parents, business people, those without school-age children, and others.

The school secretary is usually the building's hello and good-bye person. Secretaries typically greet school visitors and bid them farewell. And, they are the voices of schools -- the people who answer the phone and say, "Thank you for calling."

The school secretary is the person who sets the tone in the office, makes the boss look more efficient, eases parental concerns, soothes critics, helps students, and -- sometimes -- tends to cuts and bruises. No wonder people think of the secretary as "the school."

<u>Tips on technique</u>

- Greet people promptly and courteously. Making people feel welcome sets the tone for their entire visit.

- Most people with whom the secretary has contact are just voices on the phone. Secretaries are the same ... unless they smile while they're talking. People who smile when they're on the phone sound better, and they can take the edge off an irate caller.

- When you don't know the answer to a question, say so. Then tell callers and visitors that you'll find an answer and get back with them.

- Talk with your boss about your frustrations. Let your boss know what would make you more effective. Then ask your boss about his/her frustrations and how you can help minimize or eliminate them.

- Make a list of things you're not sure about and questions you have. Then ask your boss to help you develop some answers. Often you'll find that your boss was wondering about the same things ... or that your boss *wasn't* wondering about the same things, but is glad that you are.

- Be the epitome of confidence and loyalty. These are the things that the boss can't buy, and they're the things that every boss needs.

- Understand that you are a key source of information in your school or school district. You can correct distorted information and cut off what isn't true.

- A school secretary's day is a series of interruptions. It's common to never get around to the first thing you were going to do. Make sure that your boss understands the detours you have to take every day.

Things teachers can do

Before the first day of school, some teachers call parents to introduce them-selves. Others set a positive tone by sending informative materials home on the first day of school. A kindergarten teacher won over parents with a first-day note that said: "If you promise to believe only half of what you hear happens at school, I promise to believe only half of what I hear happens at home."

Public relations is not just another job for teachers. It's an integral part of teaching. Research indicates that the more effectively you communicate, the more competently you are perceived. There's also ample evidence that effective communication from teachers is directly related to the level of support a community provides its schools.

Experienced teachers understand the value of continuous and meaningful communication with students and their families. They know that parents who understand what is happening in the classroom are the ones most likely to provide support for the educational program.

As in the past, teachers still have to assume responsibility for communication between the classroom and the home. But now it's important that teachers do even more. They have to represent education beyond their immediate circle of students and parents, functioning as ambassadors for the education profession.

By promoting the attributes of the educational system and modeling a love for learning, teachers send an important message. And this message is di-rectly related to the quality of education in the community.

Tips on technique

■ Let people know what you do. Have a document which presents an overview of your classroom -- what you teach, who you are (a brief resume with some personal interest material sprinkled in), the focus of your class (your objectives), and the ways parents can be involved in your classroom.

■ Before school begins in the fall, contact the parents of your students. Let them know that you're looking forward to having their child in your class.

- Let parents know how they can help you help their child. Let them know what you are covering in class. Suggest home activities to reinforce what you're doing in the classroom.

- Parent-teacher conferences are one of the showcase events of the year for your classroom. Dress up your room with displays, samples of student work, and bulletin boards related to what students are currently studying.

- Consider conducting conferences with both parents and students attending. This provides parents another opportunity to be involved in their child's educational program. Provide praise for work that's well done, and solicit solutions for problems from both students and parents.

- At the elementary and middle school levels, weekly progress reports help strengthen communication with parents and students.

- Memorize a one-minute "sales pitch" for your school and public education. Use it any time you have a chance to be an ambassador for education.

- End the instructional day by summarizing what you covered. What you say at the end of the day is likely to be repeated when parents ask their children, "What did you do in school today?"

Appendix C
Marketing Plans, Techniques, and Ideas

Marketing Plans, Techniques, and Ideas
Simplified marketing planning

Marketing Plans, Techniques, and Ideas
Simplified marketing planning

We've learned that there are five steps in the marketing process -- analyze, develop strategy, plan, execute, and evaluate. In this Appendix we'll provide a practical analytical tool you can use to move your thinking from analysis to strategy, and a planning form you can use to begin developing your marketing plan. Finally, we'll provide a sample marketing plan that you can use as a guide or template for designing your own marketing initiative.

Americans always want to get moving -- to do something. We even make "to do-" lists to help us get things done. But this penchant for action may be both a strength and a fault. Launching off without a clear understanding of destination and direction usually leads to doing the wrong thing or doing the right thing poorly. The end result is the same: time and energy are wasted, and we wind up with another "to do."

You've already learned that neglecting analysis is the most frequent marketing mistake. People launch off before they have a clear understanding of the environment in which they function. This usually results in poorly conceived strategies. And poorly conceived strategy makes it difficult to develop a viable marketing plan.

To simplify both the analysis, strategy, and planning steps, Appendix C contains a building-level marketing assessment, a form that will help you analyze and develop strategy, and a one-page document which can be used to develop a marketing plan for anything.

Is your school *really* marketable?

Most principals want to market their school as a progressive, future-focused enterprise staffed by caring and competent employees. They start with the assumption that people perceive their school as a quality operation.

"We're different," they say. "We have some flaws, of course, but -- on balance -- we're a pretty good school -- good kids, good teachers, supportive parents ...."

But are your assumptions about public perceptions the reality? Do those you serve *really* see your school as you see it? Ask these key questions to find out.

❑   **Does your school provide a safe secure learning environment?**   YES 5--4--3--2--1 NO

❑   **Does your school have a competent, caring staff?**   YES 5--4--3--2--1 NO

❑   **Does your school *really* provide a quality educational program?**   YES 5--4--3--2--1 NO

❑   **Can you identify 3-5 indicators which "prove" that your school is a quality school?**   YES 5--4--3--2--1 NO

❑   **Can you and the members of your staff speak articulately about these indicators?**   YES 5--4--3--2--1 NO

❑   **Do you know what criteria people in your community use to judge your school?**   YES 5--4--3--2--1 NO

❑   **Do you and the members of staff understand your school's competitive advantage?**   YES 5--4--3--2--1 NO

❑   **Do you have a system for monitoring the external environment?**   YES 5--4--3--2--1 NO

❑   **How are learners in your school performing; i.e., can you show what your program enables students *to learn and do*?**   YES 5--4--3--2--1 NO

❑ Do you know as much as you should about those who are served by your school; i.e., your publics or customers? YES 5--4--3--2--1 NO

❑ Does your staff use test data and educational research to continuously improve? YES 5--4--3--2--1 NO

❑ Does your school have a marketing strategy? YES 5--4--3--2--1 NO

❑ Does your school have a marketing plan? YES 5--4--3--2--1 NO

❑ Do your staff members think of themselves as ambassadors for your school? YES 5--4--3--2--1 NO

❑ Do your staff members understand that they have communication and marketing responsibilities? YES 5--4--3--2--1 NO

❑ Do members of your staff know *how* to effectively communicate and market? YES 5--4--3--2--1 NO

❑ Do you use a variety of media to communicate with clearly identified target audiences? YES 5--4--3--2--1 NO

❑ Does your school look good; i.e.,

▋ are facilities well maintained YES 5--4--3--2--1 NO

▋ do staff members exude professionalism YES 5--4--3--2--1 NO

▋ are school meetings "businesslike" YES 5--4--3--2--1 NO

☐ Do staff members regularly ask themselves what value they add to the educational process?   YES 5--4--3--2--1 NO

☐ Do you regularly evaluate the effectiveness of your school?   YES 5--4--3--2--1 NO

Add the numbers you've circled.

90 and above	Outstanding
89 - 70	Ahead of the pack
69 - 50	Running with the pack
49 - 30	Panting behind the pack
29 - 0	Cleaning up after the pack

This self-assessment may be reproduced with credit to Banach, Banach & Cassidy, Inc.

Points of contact

Identifying the points of contact that various priority audiences have with your schools is a useful analytical technique which can help you develop a strategy and plan. This form is intended to help you determine if you have your best foot forward. It can also help you move toward providing contacts that are memorable for their quality.

This is analysis from a customer point of view. We've all been to places of business that left a sour taste in our mouths. The sales clerk was grumpy, the cashier was preoccupied, the isles were cluttered, the merchandise was dented, etc. At best you leave shaking your head. At worst you tell everybody you run into for the next week about your bad experience.

I have a favorite of my own. I recently pulled into a popular car wash near my home. I was the fourth car in line. As I pulled to a stop, a young girl emerged from the building to determine if those in line wanted a basic wash, an undercarriage flush, protective wax, or "the special." Then she informed those in line of the charge and collected their money. So far so good. Customers were receiving attention while they waited.

When the young girl made her way to my car, I informed her that I wanted the basic car wash. She looked at me and said, "We'll have to charge you two dollars extra because your car is dirty." All of a sudden my point of contact with the car wash took a nasty swing! "But that's why I'm here," I said. "My car is dirty and your business is washing dirty cars." This elicited no response. So I asked her if I would get a two dollar discount if my car were clean. She didn't like the question, and I decided to pull out of line and go somewhere else with my dirty car. (By the way, the people at the next car wash did a fine job, charged me the posted price, and didn't make any comments about the cleanliness of my vehicle. In fact, the attendant and the young man who towel dried the car both said, "Thanks for your business.")

Here's how to use the points of contact form to make sure you're not driving people away or leaving them in a sour mood. Use the form on the next page personally (What points of contact do people have when they are trying to reach me? The voice mail system, a secretary, a student ....) or use the form to assess the contacts people have with your school or school district (The first point of contact people have with our school is the sidewalk leading to the front door. What is the condition of the sidewalk? What messages are posted on our front door?)

First, identify your priority audiences (parents, students -- yes, students! -- business people, school volunteers, etc.). Make a copy of the points of contact-form for each priority audience. Then identify the points of contact that members of your priority audiences have with you. For each point of contact that you identify (for example, the voice mail system, the sidewalk, the front door) assign a grade of A, B, C, D, or FAIL. Then try to identify something that would make a significant improvement in each point of contact that you've identified.

Remember, it's often the little things that make a big difference. Every voice mail system can be made more user friendly, weeds growing in the sidewalk cracks can be removed, the sign on the front door can extend a welcome instead of an order to report to the office ....

Points of Contact

Priority audience _____

Points of contact	A-B-C-D-F	A significant improvement
_____	_____	_____
_____	_____	_____
_____	_____	_____
_____	_____	_____
_____	_____	_____
_____	_____	_____

ABC marketing components

The form on the next page can help you simplify the planning process. It combines -- on a single page -- the essential ingredients of a marketing plan -- objectives, positioning statement, identification of target audiences, key messages, and media, and an activities timeline.

You can use the form to develop a marketing plan for anything -- a program, a product, a service, a bond issue, or a new initiative.

Simply make a list of the things you'd like to market (Use "The marketing planner" on page 10 of Appendix A.) Then use the ABC Marketing Components form for each item on your list.

If you assemble all the components, you'll have a good start on developing a marketing plan for your school or school district. But remember what we've learned about systems theory: a system is "... a product of the interaction of its parts."

If you're charged with develop a marketing plan for your system (whether that system is a department, a building, or the school district), you'll have to assess these components within the context of the system. You'll have to determine if the components are consistent with the system's mission and vision. You'll have to assess whether all of the components complement one another, and determine if there are ways to leverage your resources. And, you'll have to decide whether it's necessary to a component or two to the plan in order to make the system work.

Here are the steps: First, identify what it is that you want to market. (*I want to market our volunteer program.*) Then, list your objectives. (*To make volunteers feel good about volunteering ... to help people understand the services provided by volunteers ... to recruit additional volunteers*) Next, it may be appropriate to ask what system priority or activity your marketing component will complement. (*This activity will complement the school district's community engagement priority.*) Four, identify the position (or identity) you hope to establish. (*Volunteering is a gift you give others ... and yourself.*) Fifth, identify the target audiences, the key messages, and the media that you'll use. (*Parents will be a key target audience. The key message will relate to how volunteers improve their child's educational program. Our media will include a brochure, parent conferences, and a newsletter article.*) Finally, develop the timeline. (*The brochure will be developed by Sam Dakota by November 1.*) Simple. Quick. Effective.

ABC Marketing Components

Here's what I'm marketing   _____

Here are my objectives   _____

_____

This will complement   _____

Here is the position I want   _____

Here are the ...

target audiences	key messages	the media
_____	_____	_____
_____	_____	_____
_____	_____	_____
_____	_____	_____

Here are the...

activities	by whom	by when
_____	_____	_____
_____	_____	_____
_____	_____	_____
_____	_____	_____

Here's an example of how to use the ABC Marketing Component-form. (This one-page marketing plan resulted in voter approval of a bond issue for a new elementary school)

WHAT I'M MARKETING
- a bond issue for a new school

MY OBJECTIVES
- to help people understand current and projected student enrollment
- to help people understand the physical condition of the current school
- to help people understand the educational need for and advantages of a new facility
- to win the election

THIS WILL COMPLEMENT
- the school district's goal of expanding quality instructional facilities

POSITION DESIRED

To position the new school as a community center which will accommodate student growth , increase instructional space, and accommodate technology, the positioning statement will be... *Building our kids' future ... today!*

TARGET	MESSAGES	MEDIA
staff	improved professional home	Staff presentations
	improved instructional space	Staff presentations
	integrated technology	Staff presentations
pre-K parents	new preschool space	Preschool teachers
	new day care space	Day care teachers
	instructional space	Parent meetings/ direct mail/phone
	integrated technology	Parent meetings/ direct mail/phone
K-6 parents	inadequacy of current facility	Next grade tours
	improved instructional space	Parent meetings/ direct mail/phone
	integrated technology	Parent meetings

ACTIVITIES	BY WHOM	BY WHEN
Develop "company line"	V.G. Writer	1 July
Develop YES voter file	C.D. Rom	1 August
Schedule staff meetings	Principal/Teacher Leader	1 August
Draft campaign literature	R.G. Writer	15 September

Of course, there were many other activities associated with winning the election, but this form provided the launch to victory.

Most people find the targets of the above campaign interesting. No messages were targeted to parents of middle and high school students, to business people, to senior citizens, and a host of other potential audiences.
The reason: Election research (Analysis is the first and most important step in the marketing process!) indicated that the bond issue would pass comfortably if one parent of every child in grades kindergarten, one, and two voted yes. To increase the odds of success, the district expanded the targeting of the campaign, aiming at parents of preschoolers, all elementary parents, and members of the school staff. The research indicated that each of these audiences ranked among the most likely to vote yes on the issue.

Quite simply, analysis revealed that the district didn't need middle and high school parents, business people, and others to win. Of course, they were kept informed about the election and the rationale for the new school, but they were not specific targets in the election. Campaign resources were targeted to the audiences which research indicated would provide a victory.

Marketing Plans, Techniques, and Ideas
Marketing at the classroom level

Marketing Plans, Techniques, and Ideas
Marketing at the classroom level

Many people believe that a school is only as good as the teacher in front of their child. We would agree.

The survey research projects we conduct around the country consistently remind us that parents are concerned first about the safety and security of their child. Once this basic concern is satisfied, parents say that the teacher in front of their child determines how they judge the school or the entire school district. They also are interested in what their child's teacher is doing in front of the class; i.e., the school program or curriculum.

The bottom line here is that the survey research findings give us insights that will help us market our schools in a very effective way -- one on one.

If the relationship between the teacher and the student is so critical to how parents judge schools, why don't we do all we can to make the relationship positive?

One technique for creating a positive relationship is called a "teacher book." As a result of our marketing academies there are now hundreds of teachers around the country who have developed these "books." Their basic purpose is to let people know who is in front of their child and what that person -- the teacher -- is doing with their child.

The teacher book is simply a standard sheet of paper folded in half. It has four panels -- a cover, two inside pages, and a back. Ideally, it should be provided to every parent at the beginning of the school year. Teacher books are inexpensive, yet one of the most effective things teachers can do.

Each of the teacher book panels is displayed on the following pages. While this is a sample template, notice that ...

- The cover extends a welcome. It makes the teacher's class sound like an exciting place. And it mentions the safety and security of the child. (After reading the cover panel, you'll probably be thinking: "I'd sure like to have this teacher in front of my child!")

• The second panel addresses a parental information need. It tells parents who is in front of their child. Notice that the brief resume mentions college degrees, but it doesn't include every inservice training program ever attended. Notice also that the brief resume shares something personal -- that the teacher has dogs and hobbies. This is important. While parents want to know that their child's teacher did graduate from college, they also want to learn that their child's teacher is "normal" -- that he/she has pets and hobbies and interests that "normal" people have. (I tell teachers: "If you don't have dogs, go out and buy some fish.")

• The third panel tells what will happen in the classroom during the year. This copy is simply a summary of what appears in your school district's curriculum guide. (If your school doesn't have a curriculum guide -- of if it's on a shelf somewhere -- here's an opportunity to establish instructional direction at the classroom and building levels.)

• The teacher book ends with suggestions on parental involvement. It helps parents understand that they are partners in their child's education, and that they have some education responsibilities.

There have been a host of reactions to the teacher book concept, all of them positive.

A teacher association president was the first to develop a teacher book in his school district. He thought it was the best communication/marketing tool that he had ever seen, and he used his association position to encourage others to develop their own teacher books.

Another teacher association president said that teachers don't like it when one teacher appears to "one-up" another. "The teacher book idea worked in our school because all teachers have one. We used a half-day inservice day, and everyone developed a book. It may have been the highest and best use of an inservice day in years."

In one district a new superintendent made teacher books a priority. After two weeks of grumbling, teachers now admit that it was the best thing they did all year. Now it's standard operating procedure -- teachers create a book the day they're hired.

Secondary teachers sometimes say that teacher books are an "elementary" idea. Not so. Both secondary students and their parents want to know who is in front of the class, and what that teacher plans to do. (In many secondary schools a student may have five or six teachers. If that's the case, use the power of technology. Get together and create an individualized book for each student. Let's students and parents know about the people on the instructional team.)

To expand on the power of personalized communication, a Michigan high school principal supplemented the teacher book idea by asking his teachers to write something on every student's report card (e.g., *Way to go!* [signed] *Mr. G.* or *Homework helps!* or *Eight weeks until finals*.). For the average teacher, this meant hand writing more than 100 comments every marking period.

"You can imagine the grumbling," said the principal. "But even I was surprised by the response. We do a number of creative things to communicate, but these simple things received more positive reaction than anything we've ever done. We don't hear grumbling any more. Teacher books and personal comments are now something that we do because our students and parents like it."

CHAMPIONS
—F O R—
CHILDREN

Welcome to Bill Banach's 4th grade classroom...

a safe, secure, exciting place where students can learn the basics and...

❏ think about things
❏ ask a lot of questions
❏ try new ideas
❏ learn from their mistakes
❏ build on their successes
❏ assume responsibility
❏ have fun

The basics and a whole lot more...Wow!

CHAMPIONS
—F O R—
CHILDREN

My name is William J. Banach. I teach 4th grade at Jefferson Elementary School. My friends call me Bill.

I prepared for teaching by attending Northern Michigan, Michigan State, and Western Michigan. These universities granted my Bachelors, Masters, and Doctorate Degrees. My initial training was in speech pathology with a focus in elementary education. I've been an educator for 25 years.

It seems as if I began student teaching yesterday. Now, a quarter century later, I enjoy teaching as much -- maybe more! -- than the day I started. I love working with children, and am proud of my profession. I believe I'm making a contribution to the future *every day*.

My colleagues often call me creative and caring. My students might add the word demanding. They're both right.

I'm married and have four children -- two boys and two girls. We live in the woods with our three dogs -- Kahuna, Newton, and Cassidy.

I enjoy a lot of things -- flying, reading, photography, skeet shooting, boating, fishing, and gadgets of all kinds. I like doing things with my family more than anything. Being with my students is a close second.

We're going to have a great year!

Here are some of the things we expect to cover in 4th grade

In language arts students will ... experience a variety of literature • read novels, short stories, legends, poems, and biographies • identify fact and opinion • correctly spell grade level words • use reference and resource materials • sharpen their writing skills • edit and publish their writing • listen critically and constructively • use their reading, writing, and speaking skills in everything they do

In mathematics students will ... increase their multiplication and division skills • be introduced to long division • solve equations with missing signs • add and subtract decimals • use calculators for addition, subtraction, multiplication, and division • recognize types of angles • apply math skills to real life situations • construct bar, line, and picture graphs

In science students will ... observe the forces that affect the rate of change • recognize that objects do not have to touch to exert force on one another • explore the properties of magnetism • learn that energy takes many forms • discover how atmospheric change affects the earth's weather and our lives • observe how living things interact with each other and their physical environment

In history and social studies, students will ... learn the role Michiganders played in U.S. history • learn about the history, geography, topography, and government of Michigan • learn about important Michiganders, past and present • become aware of civic responsibilities • learn how to resolve conflict

All this ... *and a whole lot more!*

Being a partner in your child's education is as easy as A, B, C

A. Be involved. Know what your child is studying. Keep yourself tuned in. (We have a weekly parent letter and a student-generated web page -- www.wow!.com -- to keep you posted.

B. Don't be a "wonderer" -- *wondering* what's going on or *wondering* why something is happening. Call. Ask a question, express a concern, suggest a solution, or share an idea. You can reach me at school (784.9352). The best time is between 7:30 and 8 a.m. or between 1 and 2 p.m. You can e-mail me anytime at wbanach@go.four.it.k-12.mi.us or you can call me at home (784.9353) after 7 p.m. any evening.

C. Understand that fourth graders do have homework. Don't ask your child *if* there's homework. Ask your child *what* today's homework assignment is and *when* he or she will have it completed. Ask if you can help. Then check to see that the homework is done.

[Below is where you can put your school/school district logo and mission statement. Don't forget to include your address and telephone number (with area code).

BANACH, BANACH & CASSIDY
O U T S I D E   I N S I G H T

Banach, Banach & Cassidy, 21969 Cimarron Lane, Ray Township, MI 48096
810.784.9888 • Fax 810.784.8412
We do everything that has anything to do with communication.

Here's another suggestion for panel four

Want some extra credit?

<u>You can help your child with writing</u> by encouraging your child to write notes, lists, letters, and journals -- anything! Remind your child to proof-read. Help your child master spelling words.

<u>You can help your child with science</u> by talking about what we're doing in science. You can supplement this by exploring other resources (videos, books, games, the Internet, etc.). Consider science kits as gifts.

<u>You can help your child in reading</u> by encouraging your child to read alone or aloud for 20 minutes every day -- after chores and before TV. Have your child tell you about what he has read.

<u>You can help your child develop good listening and speaking skills</u> by modeling these skills. Encourage memorization of poems, rhymes, oral reports ... even jokes.

People say parents are a child's first teacher, and no one disputes how important parents are to the growth and development of their child. However, some parents are tempted to dump responsibility for their child's education on the schoolhouse door. Don't do that. You're my partner in your child's fourth grade educational program. Working together, we can be unbeatable. And when that happens, guess who wins?

BANACH, BANACH & CASSIDY
O U T S I D E   I N S I G H T

Banach, & Cassidy, 21969 Cimarron Lane, Ray Township, MI 48096
810.784.9888 • Fax 810.784.8412
We do everything that has anything to do with communication.

Following up ... every week!

Here's one way to maintain the one-on-one relationship with parents. It's a weekly progress report -- a half page sent home very Friday. (Some teachers prefer every Monday because it gives them the weekend, and because students and parents tend to lose things in the Friday shuffle.)

This progress report is easy and effective. It works best if you add a handwritten comment; e.g., *Johnny had a great week!* or *Have Kelsey tell you about her science test.* This progress report provides the information that parents want. It's the kind of thing effective teachers do. And it's great marketing!

CHAMPIONS
—F O R—
CHILDREN

This is the week that was!

All things considered, _____

had a week that was   ❏ great
                      ❏ good
                      ❏ so-so
                      ❏ not too good

<u>class work was</u>

satisfactory   in need of improvement   unsatisfactory

<u>behavior was</u>

satisfactory   in need of improvement   unsatisfactory

Comments:_____

My child and I discussed this. Parent signature _____

Please have your child return this to school tomorrow. Thanks.

Appendix D
A Framework for the Future

A Framework for the Future

During the mid-1990s Banach, Banach & Cassidy, Inc. helped design and facilitate a planning and marketing initiative for a regional education agency (intermediate school district) in Michigan. The goal was to identify the "common ground" which existed among local school districts served by the regional agency, and to develop a guide to planning for the future.

The document that emerged from this initiative was titled *A Framework for the Future*.

This initiative has now been replicated in a number of regional agencies, and is outlined here because ...

- It demonstrates how The Market-Driven System® (MDS) can be amended to address a specific need or objective.

- It demonstrates that school districts can leverage their resources if their leaders commit to cooperating.

- It provides an example of the leadership which regional education agencies are uniquely positioned to provide.

- It showcases common sense.

- It can create a preferred future for everyone involved.

All *Frameworks* have been initiated at the superintendent level. And their effectiveness seems directly correlated with the commitment and tenacity of the superintendent.

As is the case with MDS planning, the process begins with an analysis of the change forces which have potential for impacting the agency and its constituent districts. The process usually begins with a meeting of the regional and constituent (local) district superintendents, although others may be involved.

Following the analysis, participants are asked to reflect on education in the region and to respond to three questions (using the form in Appendix A titled, "What's wrong, right, and wonderful?"):

1. What's wrong and needs to be fixed?

2. What's okay and needs to be maintained?

3. What's wonderful and ought to be expanded?

Next, the superintendents are asked to identify those needs and opportunities which they have in common. These become the "dimensions" of their *Framework for the Future.*

The meeting ends when those involved feel comfortable with the draft list of dimensions. (Our experience has been that the entire meeting will take about four or five hours.)

After the meeting the facilitator drafts the dimensions and sends them to the regional superintendent who, in turn, shares them with the constituent superintendents. Recipients of the draft are invited to make changes or additions, and to discuss the dimensions at a subsequent meeting.

Once the dimensions are agreed upon, a writer can begin drafting a *Framework* document; i.e., developing some copy related to the dimensions and preparing a booklet for use in communicating the thinking.

Extending the process to the staff and community engagement phase requires a regional and local district dissemination plan. Implementation of the dissemination plan should start internally (for example, with school boards, principals, school staff) and move externally (for example, to parents, service groups, the business community, etc.). At each step of the dissemination process, it's important to ...

- reinforce the economic and strategic sensibility of cooperation.

- present the *Framework* as a guide to planning. (Stress that the *Framework* is designed to evolve as school districts make progress toward their visions and adjust to accommodate environmental changes.)

- invite people to strengthen the thinking contained in the *Framework*. (Ask people to tell you what they like most , and to share what bothers them. Then ask them to share their thinking on any or all of the dimensions.)

The sample materials which follow exhibit key elements of the *Framework* process. The samples also provide a variety of approaches to cooperative planning which demonstrate the flexibility of The Market-Driven System®. On the following pages you'll find sample *Framework* text, planning materials which demonstrate how a regional agency can use this process to develop or enhance its own strategic plan (again, using an adaptation of The Market-Driven System®), and techniques for engaging people in the process.

A *Framework for the Future* document

Here is the cover page for the *Framework for the Future* document prepared for the Charlevoix-Emmet Intermediate School District in Michigan. Note that this introduction establishes the document as a guide to planning, and reinforces the sensibility of cooperation.

> No one knows what the future will bring. And no one can say -- with any certainty -- what tomorrow might look like.
>
> But there are numerous forces driving change, and a host of indicators that tell us tomorrow will be different than today.
>
> This is what makes planning for the future difficult -- we know that things will be different, but we don't know all the ways in which they'll be different.
>
> That's why the local school districts in the Charlevoix-Emmet service area have developed this *Framework for the Future*. The *Framework* is a guide to planning a better tomorrow. It is a living document which is designed to be changed as the operating environment changes. In short, the *Framework* is intended to provide direction for the future while giving local school districts the flexibility they need to capitalize on change.
>
> Preparation of this document began with some questions about the future and a look across the service area. Education leaders discussed the kinds of programs and services needed by students

... they talked about integrating technology into the schools ...
they stressed the importance of human interaction in the learning
process ... and they talked about the economic and strategic sensibility
of working together in the best interests of all students.

It didn't take long to reach consensus on the need to engage
school staff and members of the community in this discussion.
Everyone believed that the success of all local school districts was
dependent on developing a broad-based understanding of change
and its implications in all local school districts. In fact, this
belief provided the impetus to bring people together to define
the dimensions of an education within the context of an
environment characterized by continuous change.

You're invited to take part in this journey toward the future.
Think about the dimensions highlighted in this document.
Then share your thoughts with us so that the *Framework* can
become a document which reflects everyone's best thinking.
The thinking we do and the dialog we have are important first
steps to creating an exciting future for all learners in the
Charlevoix-Emmet ISD service area.

This "cover copy" is followed by the dimensions identified by the local school
district superintendents. To help you visualize the format of the document,
here are two dimensions and the explanatory paragraphs from the Charlevoix-Emmet *Framework for the Future*:

Dimensions of the Framework for the Future
Charlevoix-Emmet ISD

1. <u>To design and implement a cooperative initiative to
build better understanding of and support for public schools</u>

Public understanding is crucial to building, maintaining, and
improving quality educational opportunities. That's why an
informed citizenry is in the best interest of schools ... *and* the
people they serve. In fact, helping people understand specific
school programs and services is an important local district
responsibility.

Yet, there are numerous ways to cooperatively address topics which are common in all school districts. For example, all school districts can help themselves by working together to help people understand topics such as the importance of education, the future needs of learners, business-government-education partnerships, funding, career opportunities, and others. The focus of this initiative will be to identify topical areas which are common to all school districts, and to develop a plan to communicate about them across the area.

2. To integrate instructional and communication technologies into the school program.

Technology has influenced our daily learning the same way it has influenced our daily living. And, as has been the case in our daily living, technology is more useful and beneficial to students when it's integrated into the learning process -- when it's a transparent part of our daily learning. The emphasis in this dimension will be to view technology as an important tool for enhancing our human capacity, and to use technology in ways that improve our thinking and understanding.

After stating all of the dimensions, the Charlevoix-Emmet ISD's *Framework* document concludes with an invitation to strengthen the thinking:

This *Framework for the Future* requires new thinking. All of us have to think about what is good for our school district *and* other school districts in the area.

In fact, capitalizing on the forces of radical change may require every school district to give a little to get a lot for all learners in the area.

The emphasis on cooperating promises broadened educational opportunities for all learners in the area. And -- truth be told -- cooperative delivery of educational programs is coming whether we like it or not. It is being driven by two powerful forces: technology and a school funding system that was designed to equalized educational opportunities across Michigan.

By working together we can get ahead of the change while creating more opportunities for our schools and the people they serve. We can do that by journeying toward the future cooperatively, and by using the dimensions outlined in this *Framework* as our launch pad.

What do you think?

Framework feedback

Whenever a *Framework* document is presented, there's an opportunity for engagement and feedback that shouldn't be missed. It's easy to provide an audience with a few questions designed to stimulate discussion or to be returned in writing. These questions appear in a single sheet questionnaire developed for use at the Traverse Bay Area Intermediate School District in Michigan. Every agency with a *Framework* document has used them to strategic advantage.

What do you think?

1. Which dimension of the *Framework for the Future* do you particularly like ... and why is that?

2. Which dimension raises questions or concerns ... and what are they?

3. If you could add another dimension to the *Framework for the Future*, what would it be?

4. Help us strengthen our thinking. Please comment on any or all of the dimensions.

Thank you.

A *Framework* document provides a strong foundation for cooperative educational programming. It also helps regional education services agencies serve their constituent school districts. And, it can provide the impetus for a regional educational service agency to reassess its role in a period of radical change.

For example, at Charlevoix-Emmet ISD, Superintendent Mark Eckhardt enhanced the *Framework* process by assembling his administrative cabinet for a retreat focused on the role and function of the intermediate school district. That retreat began with a review of the *Framework* and an assessment of the needs of the agency's constituent school districts. In that context, Eckhardt asked his administrators to address four questions:

1. What do we do well at Charlevoix-Emmet?

2. What do we need to improve?

3. What do we need to add?

4. What do we need to ditch; i.e, stop doing?

(Eckhardt and his staff later expanded this assessment by meeting with each constituent school district's administrative staff to assess their needs.)

The four-question assessment was followed by a discussion of the regional agency's role in the context of radical change. The discussion resulted in the development of a new vision, mission, and statement of priorities for the agency. These items are presented below to demonstrate how one regional agency capitalized on radical change by leading its local districts toward a preferred future.

Notice also that the vision and mission are one sentence in length, and that both statements are clear, concise ... and powerful.

CHARLEVOIX-EMMET ISD STATEMENT OF VISION

*It is the vision of the Charlevoix-Emmet ISD to be
an indispensable part of every local school
district it serves.*

In pursuit of this vision, the Charlevoix-Emmet ISD will ...

- create a culture of marked by openness, trust, and innovation
- proactively pursue educational opportunities for learners of all ages
- focus on helping local school districts be successful
- build an environment where everyone is learning

CHARLEVOIX-EMMET ISD STATEMENT OF MISSION

*It is the mission of the Charlevoix-Emmet ISD
to serve local school districts.*

To fulfill this mission, the Charlevoix-Emmet ISD will ...

- employee a competent and caring staff
- continually monitor local school district needs
- seek opportunities in the marketplace on behalf of local school districts
- provide the highest quality leadership at every operating level

CHARLEVOIX-EMMET ISD PRIORITIES

1. To design and implement a plan to market Charlevoix-Emmet ISD programs and services.

2. To identify common service needs of local school districts and implement a plan for their delivery.

3. To develop, disseminate, and process the dimensions of the *Framework for the Future*.

4. To design, develop, and implement an internal and external communication infrastructure plan.

5. To identify and begin the delivery of alternative education programs which serve local school districts.

6. To facilitate development of calendars and contract provisions which support cooperative education programs and services.

The St. Clair Intermediate School District is another regional education service agency that is using the *Framework* process. Superintendent Joe Caimi began the process with a survey of educators served by his agency and a school board planning session. Now he meets with his local district superintendents to identify their individual priorities and to discuss the educational "common ground" in the agency's service area.

Caimi's administrative team evaluates the information provided by local district superintendents. Then they schedule face-to-face meetings with every building principal in their service area. Members of the administrative staff divide up the list of principals and arrange individual interviews to determine which of the agency's services are most valued by principals and to ascertain how the agency can help each principal address his/her priorities.

While these personal interviews are time consuming, Caimi thinks they're important. "Principals have a lot of power," he says. "If our agency is going to have a positive effect on educational change, we have to have the principals as partners. And that means addressing their needs and serving them well."

Not surprisingly, local district principals appreciate the personal interviews. While the administrators gathered information which would help improve the regional agency's programming, they simultaneously enhanced perceptions of the regional agency's responsiveness. At the same time, the ISD administrators gained first-hand insight into building-level problems and priorities., and, in turn, reinforced the importance of staying "close to the customer."

Superintendent Mike McIntyre of the Traverse Bay Area Intermediate School District (TBA ISD) created the first *Framework for the Future*. It is the guiding document for every activity at his regional education service agency.

McIntyre reports that implementing the *Framework* has been hard work. But he'll quickly add that he can't think of anything more important to have on his agenda. "Quite simply," he says, "we're here to serve local school districts. And our *Framework* process sustains itself by keeping us focused on better ways of doing things together for the benefit of everyone. It has made us much more effective as an agency, and much more valuable to the local school districts we serve."

Dimensions of a *Framework for the Future*

The following dimensions have been identified by school districts participating in the *Framework* process. These are commonly identified areas of "common ground." They are the things which superintendents and others believe school districts can work on cooperatively to the benefit of everyone. Use them to jump start your thinking ... and to begin identifying the common ground in your regional education service agency's service area.

- To engage the staff and community in defining the dimensions of an educational program.

- To develop and implement a plan for integrating technology into all facets of school operation.

- To develop and implement a plan for developing, enhancing, and articulating the K-12 curriculum.

- To align student assessments, and design and implement a competency-based diploma system.

- To reassess the special education delivery system and funding formula.

- To insure that all students have access to a core educational program.

- To investigate the feasibility of nontraditional school structures and instructional delivery systems (e.g., virtual classrooms).

- To develop policies and procedures which support and enhance cooperative programming.

- To develop employee contracts and calendars which support flexible scheduling options.

- To develop a vision, mission, and priorities for alternative education programs such as adult education, community education, programming for at-risk students, etc.

- To investigate the feasibility of cooperatively delivering educational support services.

- To develop and implement a vision related staff development program.

- To create community partnerships which enhance teaching and learning.

- To cooperatively market public education programs.

- To seek grants and pursue alternative funding sources.

Creating cooperation

Things are changing for every organization. Certainly regional education agencies are no exception. In fact, the forces of radical change are dramatically altering the roles of these agencies.

By addressing their constituent districts' needs and wants, regional education agencies can position themselves at the leading edge of change. By seizing a leadership position they can positively affect teaching and learning. And -- at a more basic level -- exercising leadership will enable them to remain in business.

To assure that your regional education agency serves its clients effectively and efficiently, follow these steps to creating a framework for your agency:

1. Define the emerging context. Identify the dimensions of the internal and external environments which must be acknowledged and accommodated. Then think about their implications for your agency.

2. Select a model for thinking and planning strategically. Use or adapt a model (such as The Market-Driven System®) which will provide the strategic flexibility *you* need at *your* agency.

3. Identify the critical issues. Learn which issues have potential for impacting public education and the issues which are on *your* horizon.

4. Design a framework for pursuing fundamental change. Identify the dimensions which need to be accommodated in implementing fundamental change at *your* agency.

5. Initiate internal dialogue on priorities and action. In a collegial and nonconfrontational way, facilitate honest discussions about the way things ought to be at *your* agency.

6. Move the dialogue to key external audiences. Identify the people who can enhance *your* agency's thinking and planning.

7. Build coalitions for change. Form the alliances which are in the best interests of learners served by *your* agency.